About the Author

BHAGIRATH LAL DAS served in the Indian Administrative Service, from where he retired as a Secretary to the Government of India. He has had a long association with international trade issues, participating directly in a large number of bilateral and multilateral trade negotiations. He was India's Ambassador and Permanent Representative to GATT and Deputy Permanent Representative to UNCTAD in Geneva. During that period he also functioned as Chairman of the GATT Council and of the GATT Contracting Parties. Later he spent five years with UNCTAD as its Director of International Trade Programmes. In that capacity, along with his other responsibilities, he organised and coordinated UNCTAD's technical assistance programme for developing countries to facilitate their participation in the Uruguay Round of Multilateral Trade Negotiations which culminated in the setting up of the World Trade Organisation. He now provides consultancy services to various institutions.

The WTO Agreements: Deficiencies, Imbalances and Required Changes

Bhagirath Lal Das

Zed Books Ltd.
London and New York

TWN
Third World Network
Penang, Malaysia

The WTO Agreements: Deficiencies, Imbalances and Required Changes
is published by
Zed Books Ltd., 7 Cynthia Street,
London N1 9JF, UK and Room 400,
175 Fifth Avenue, New York,
NY 10010, USA
and
Third World Network,
228 Macalister Road,
10400 Penang, Malaysia.

Distributed in the USA exclusively by
St. Martin's Press, Inc.,
175 Fifth Avenue, New York,
NY 10010, USA.

Cover design by C-Square

Printed by Jutaprint, 2 Solok Sungai Pinang 3,
11600 Penang, Malaysia.

ISBN: 1 85649 583 3 Hb
ISBN: 1 85649 584 1 Pb

A catalogue record for this book is obtainable from the British Library.

US CIP has been applied for from the Library of Congress.

To my father

Pandit Shree Madhava Lal Das

TERMS USED:

The terms "country", "countries", "Member country" and "Member countries" occur sometimes in the text. These terms have been used for simplicity and convenience, though it is well recognised that the territories of some Members of the WTO may not fit exactly into this category.

CONTENTS

PREFACE

THE close of the Uruguay Round of Multilateral Trade Negotiations was followed by massive publicity on the part of several institutions about the impressive benefits which would be the outcome of the negotiations. This was aimed at smoothening the process of acceptance of the decisions by various governments. The negotiators and trade policy officials were congratulating themselves on the excellent results they had achieved and the manner in which they had protected the vital interests of their respective countries. There was no time for all those directly involved in the negotiations to pause to think about the severely uneven nature of the Agreements. Those pointing out such aberrations were either ignored or branded as spoil-sports with a negative attitude. Unfortunately this was so even in developing countries.

Yet this has been a unique negotiation in which most of the concessions were made by developing countries without getting anything but meagre concessions in return. This is not because the negotiators or the trade policy officials of developing countries ignored the interests of their countries. In fact some of them set excellent examples as consummate negotiators and mature officials. In spite of their best capabilities they could not influence the course of negotiations except in very marginal ways here and there. The results of this round of the MTNs are, in fact, characterised by the massive gap between the economic and political strengths of developed and developing countries. The latter found themselves in an extremely vulnerable position and succumbed to bilateral and multilateral pressures. Perhaps they could have limited the damage, if they had been together; but this round also saw the collapse of coordination among the developing countries.

The Uruguay Round results did bring about some important improvements in the GATT system as explained at various places in this book; but this should not make us lose sight of the deficiencies and imbalances in the Agreements flowing out of this round.

Now the developing countries have the experience of about two years of the implementation of the WTO Agreements. It is time they had a look at the Agreements again, particularly with two objectives. First, they should perhaps ponder over the reasons why they had to make all these concessions without commensurate returns. This may help them to identify their strengths and weaknesses and provide objective lessons for deciding on future strategies. Second, it will be useful for them to examine the deficiencies and imbalances in the WTO Agreements from their points of view and make efforts to bring about desirable changes in them. The modest exercise in this book addresses itself to the second objective.

First, the book gives an account of the severe overall imbalance in the concessions made by the developing countries and the developed countries in the Uruguay Round results. It also discusses how the recent trend in the WTO is towards enhancing the imbalance, rather than taking corrective steps to reduce it. Thereafter specific subjects are taken up for discussion and analysis. Beginning with the enforcement of rights and obligations, i.e., the dispute settlement process, which is one of the main achievements of the Uruguay Round, the book goes on to the market access covering tariffs and grey area measures, followed by contingency trade measures which cover balance of payment measures and safeguards. The next chapter discusses the measures against unfair trade practices, i.e., subsidies and dumping. Then the agreements in specific sectors, like agriculture and textiles, are taken up. There follows a chapter on non-traditional issues, viz., services and intellectual property rights. The next chapter deals with a topical subject, i.e., neo-protectionism and then a forgotten-yet-important subject, i.e., the commitments of developed countries in Part IV of GATT 1994. Finally there is a discussion on the suitability of the current environment for initiatives from developing countries and the desirable strategies to be followed.

Each of the chapters on specific subjects, from the enforcement of rights and obligations to the sectoral agreements, is divided into four sections: a brief description of the relevant agreements, an account of the improvements and the positive features, deficiencies and imbalances and finally the required changes. A consolidated summary of positive features, deficiencies and imbalances, and required changes is given in the last chapter.

It must be appreciated that the perception of deficiencies and imbalances depends on the points of reference of the viewer. The elements which are considered as examples of deficiency by some persons or countries may be taken to be perfectly normal and desirable by others. And since there were diverse interests in these negotiations which were sometimes even adversarial, it is natural not to expect unanimity on the identification of deficiencies and imbalances. The current exercise focuses on developing countries, keeping their interests and perspective in mind.

At this stage it may be relevant to address the important issue as to whether one can talk of the interests of developing countries as a group. It is often argued that the diversity among them is so wide that it is not relevant to consider them as one entity. But it should be realised that although the developed countries forming the OECD are also greatly diverse in their economic characteristics and stature, we consider them as a group of countries while describing and analysing various features. Further, even within any particular country, there are widely differing interests in respect of any issue, and yet one talks of the interest of that country as a whole on a particular subject.

Developing countries with all their diversities share certain common handicaps, though there may be some exceptions. A very large number of them have intrinsic economic weaknesses. They are also technologically weak. Resources devoted to research and development in these countries are small and their share in industrial innovations is negligible compared to those in developed countries. Their infrastructure for manufacture and trade as well as modern services is weak. They are short of resources for investment in these areas. All these handicaps indicate bleak prospects not only for the present but also in the near future.

Apart from such rationale as mentioned above for considering developing countries as a group, there is another more formal reason for doing so. GATT and WTO Agreements recognise developing countries as specific entities (as less developed contracting parties in GATT and as developing country Members in WTO Agreements) and, as such, their being considered as a group in the context of an analysis relating to GATT and WTO Agreements appears very reasonable.

One of the various aspects of the weakness of developing countries is reflected in their participation in the WTO negotiations. Though some of their representatives have been making arduous efforts individually, their preparation is in general weak and their resources, including the personnel resources, are overstretched because of very heavy demands by a series of formal and informal meetings and discussions going on in the WTO simultaneously.

It is hoped that the efforts made in this book will provide these overworked ladies and gentlemen with some food for thought regarding their approach and priorities in the WTO negotiations and discussions in future. The relevance and utility of this exercise may be wider if those directly or indirectly concerned with the international trade policy issues pause to give a passing look at this "other view" on the results of the Uruguay Round which have generally received wide acclamation in several quarters.

The real inspiration for writing this text came from Martin Khor Kok Peng of the Third World Network. I had noticed the deficiencies and imbalances in the WTO Agreements while preparing for UNCTAD a detailed course material on the WTO for the training of developing countries' trade officials and the executives of trade and industry. But it did not strike me at that time that a compilation of these observations would be really useful. It was the persistence of Martin which made me give serious thought to the possibility of preparing a text like the present one. I thank him sincerely for initiating this venture.

Bhagirath Lal Das

CHAPTER 1

MAJOR IMBALANCES IN THE URUGUAY ROUND RESULTS

THE LAUNCH OF THE URUGUAY ROUND

TOWARDS the end of 1983, the United States and Japan made a joint declaration in Tokyo that serious thought should be given to preparing a new round of multilateral trade negotiations in the General Agreement on Tariffs and Trade (GATT). Though initially the European Economic Community was not enthusiastic, as it was apprehensive that the negotiations would focus on the liberalisation in agriculture, it finally gave its support to the proposal. The matter was intensely followed up by the major industrialised countries. The developing countries did not support the launch of a new round of negotiations in GATT mainly because of their fear on three counts, viz.: (i) they would be the main targets for extracting concessions in any new round, (ii) new subjects of interest to developed countries in which the developing countries themselves had no particular interest would be taken up for negotiations, and (iii) the subjects which had been of interest to them for a long time would get ignored, as the focus in GATT would shift to the new issues initiated in the round.

A preparatory process started in GATT, and a new round of Multilateral Trade Negotiations (MTNs), called the Uruguay Round, was launched in Punta del Este, a sea resort in Uruguay, towards the end of 1986.

EARLIER ROUNDS OF MTNS

Several rounds of Multilateral Trade Negotiations had been completed earlier. All these, except the Tokyo Round (which was concluded in 1979 and was the immediate predecessor of the Uruguay Round), concentrated on negotiations for reduction of tariffs (customs duties). The Tokyo Round covered reduction of tariffs and also several subjects outside tariffs (usually called non-tariff measures, NTMs) which affect imports and exports. A number of agreements were concluded in that round which have been commonly called the Tokyo Round Codes. These codes were not universally applicable to all members of GATT; they were applicable only to those members that accepted them.

Almost immediately after the completion of the Tokyo Round at the end of 1979, major industrialised countries started feeling that their interest extended far beyond merely the trade in goods, which had been the traditional subject of GATT. For example, the international transaction in services sectors, the protection of intellectual property rights, particularly the protection of patents, and more free and secure opportunities for their investors were considered to be of immense importance for their economies. Also some major industrialised countries and important exporters of agricultural products among the developing countries were keen on introducing more discipline in the agriculture sector, which had earlier remained under a soft discipline in GATT.

With these expectations as a background, the Uruguay Round was launched. It was finally concluded in the middle of 1994 with a Ministerial Meeting in Marrakesh which established the World Trade Organisation (WTO) and finalised the WTO Agreements which finally came into effect on 1 January 1995.

THE FAMILY OF WTO AGREEMENTS

The WTO Agreements subsume the old GATT with all the amendments and decisions taken by it till 31 December 1994. In Marrakesh, some Understandings were reached on clarifications, interpretations and elaborations regarding certain provisions of GATT. The old

GATT, along with the earlier amendments and decisions till 31 December 1994 and these new Understandings, is collectively now called GATT 1994 and it forms a part of the family of WTO Agreements.

This family also includes elaborate agreements on twelve subjects in the area of goods, viz., agriculture, sanitary and phytosanitary measures, textiles and clothing, technical barriers to trade, trade-related investment measures, anti-dumping, customs valuation, pre-shipment inspection, rules of origin, import licensing, subsidies and countervailing measures and safeguards.

It also contains agreements in the areas of services, intellectual property rights, trade policy review mechanisms and dispute settlement processes.

Further, it contains four plurilateral agreements, one each in the areas of government procurement, civil aircraft, dairy and bovine meat.

The four plurilateral agreements are applicable only to those countries which have accepted them. All the other agreements of the family of WTO Agreements mentioned above apply to all Members of the WTO.

IMBALANCES IN CONCESSIONS AND COMMITMENTS

In these negotiations all countries have made concessions as is customary in multilateral trade negotiations. But a significant feature of the Uruguay Round is that developing countries have made far more concessions than they have received. Several quantitative assessments have been attempted to measure the loss or gain of various countries or groups of countries; but these suffer from the usual handicaps of uncertain assumptions and methodologies of modelling. Hence it is no surprise that there have been wide variations in the results of these assessments. One relevant measure of the balance of concessions and commitments in these negotiations could be a comparison of the rights and obligations of the Members before the beginning of the Uruguay Round and those after the coming into force of the WTO Agreements.

A careful overall comparison suggests that most of the concessions and commitments have come from developing countries and very few from industrialised countries.

Let us first take the important concessions and commitments of developed countries which may be of benefit to the developing countries. In agriculture, developed countries have made commitments to reduce their import restrictions, domestic support and export subsidies by 20 to 36% (over the levels in 1986-88) during the five years after 1 January 1995. Though there are some specific problems in this regard which will be discussed in the chapter on sectoral issues, these measures will, no doubt, improve the market access in these countries in the area of agriculture. To that extent, those developing countries that are exporters of agricultural products will derive benefit.

Another sector of importance is textiles. Here, the developed countries have committed to eliminate the special restrictive regimes which were coming on for more than three decades in the form of Multi-Fibre Agreements. This commitment is qualified by certain drawbacks which will be explained in the chapter on sectoral issues. However, the commitment to abolish the special import regime in this sector is quite significant for those developing countries that are exporters of textiles and clothing.

In the areas of contingent action and unfair trade, like safeguards, countervailing duties for subsidies and anti-dumping, a certain degree of objectivity has been introduced and there are provisions for *de minimis* limits for exemption from action. These will benefit developing countries as they have often been subjected to repeated actions in these areas, particularly in the area of anti-dumping.

Grey area measures, i.e., selective quantitative restrictions in some sectors of particular interest to developing countries, have been prohibited in future, and existing measures will be terminated in a definite time frame.

The enforcement of rights and obligations through the dispute settlement process has been improved mainly on two counts. First, the discretion of a country to block action against it has been curtailed; and second, time-limits have been prescribed for various stages of the dispute settlement process. This is a significant improvement for a weak trading partner like a developing country.

As against these commitments of developed countries which are important for developing countries, let us consider the commitments and concessions which have been made by the developing countries. Some of the important ones are listed below.

(i)   Several developing countries have made huge reductions in their tariffs and bound them, i.e., they have committed not to raise them beyond specified levels. For example, a calculation made after the conclusion of the Uruguay Round indicates that India's trade-weighted average tariff on industrial products has been reduced from 71.4% to 32.4%, Brazil's from 40.6% to 27%, Chile's from 34.9% to 24.9%, Mexico's from 46.1% to 33.7%, Venezuela from 50% to 30.9% etc. As against this picture, the average trade-weighted tariff on industrial products for developed countries has been reduced from 6.3% to 3.8%.

One may argue that the tariffs of developing countries were very high earlier, and it was thus only reasonable that they should have been reduced. This point will be discussed in detail in the chapter on market access. The fact however remains that the average reduction of tariff during the Uruguay Round has been much steeper in several developing countries compared to the reduction in developed countries.

(ii)   Subsidy for production and export was earlier recognised as a valid instrument of development in developing countries; and thus they were able to use subsidies as permissible means to encourage production and export. But now the developing countries, except those having per capita GNP of US$1,000 or less per annum, have committed to eliminate the existing subsidies over a specified time period and also not to use subsidies later.

(iii)   Earlier, the developing countries were allowed to impose direct quantitative restrictions on import, if they faced balance of payment problems. Now they have agreed that direct quantitative restrictions will be applied only if tariff-type measures are not adequate to deal with their balance of payment problems. Though there was a certain degree of priority for tariff-type measures even earlier, it has now been made much more explicit and rigid.

(iv)   In the anti-dumping cases, the role of the panels formed in the dispute settlement process has been severely curtailed, which will be discussed in detail in the chapters on enforcement of rights and obligations and on unfair trade practices. Considering that developing countries have been frequent targets of anti-dumping actions by developed countries, they have really made a significant concession by agreeing to make the dispute settlement process quite ineffective in this important sector.

(v)   Developing countries have agreed to include services in the framework of WTO Agreements and thereby they have agreed to take part in the liberalisation of the services sector. The degree of concession made by the developing countries in including the sector of services in the WTO system can be gauged from the stiff resistance they put up against including this subject in the agenda of the Uruguay Round. In this subject, the demand and intense pressure for the negotiation was from the developed countries.

(vi)   Developing countries have agreed to include the standards of intellectual property rights, particularly the patents rights, in the framework of WTO Agreements. In this area also, the demand for the negotiation was from the developed countries.

(vii)   In agreeing to include these two subjects in the negotiations and later in the WTO framework, developing countries have made a major concession of a vital nature, as they have now opened the door for similar new subjects in future.

(viii)   Developed countries had put up a demand for cross-retaliation in the dispute settlement process, whereby action could be taken against a country in some area for lapses in another area. Developing countries have agreed to include this provision in the agreement which will mostly operate against them, as will be explained in detail in the chapter on enforcement of rights and obligations.

One can go on adding to this list. These are only some of the important and obvious examples.

DEMAND FOR NEW CONCESSIONS

One of the main objectives of the developed countries in starting the new round of negotiations of multilateral trade negotiations in GATT (which was later named as the Uruguay Round) was to extract concessions and commitments from developing countries. And in this they did succeed. The illustrative list mentioned above would indicate that it has been a strange example of totally unbalanced international negotiations in which a set of countries, viz., the developing countries, had to make most of the concessions, and the other group, viz., the developed countries made very little concessions of relevance to the former.

And yet the demand on the developing countries for further concessions has not stopped. Hardly a year had passed after the coming into force of the results of these negotiations, when major developed countries started putting pressure for negotiations in new areas, with the obvious objective of getting further new commitments from developing countries. Some of these important areas are easier trade action for environmental reasons, inclusion of labour rights in the framework of the WTO and curtailment of the rights of the host countries in guiding foreign investment in their jurisdiction.

The Member countries of the WTO have yet to grasp fully the impact of the Uruguay Round Agreements on their economies. In fact several of them have yet to study the problems of the implementation of these agreements. One would have thought it to be wise to let these new agreements, which are of far-reaching nature, to consolidate before embarking on new series of trade negotiations. But the major industrialised countries are clearly in a hurry to consolidate their own gains and to push ahead further with their agenda in new areas of their interest.

CONSIDERATION OF DEFICIENCIES AND IMBALANCES

In this context it becomes relevant for developing countries to examine the deficiencies and imbalances in the current agreements and propose their own agenda for the negotiations in the near future, with the objective of removing these deficiencies and imbalances and improving the operation of the agreements. And there are numerous such features in the agreements, as explained in subsequent chapters, which need immediate attention.

Surely when altogether new issues are being pressed for negotiation by the major developed countries, it is quite reasonable for the developing countries to come up with their own proposals for improving the existing agreements. The chapters which follow list some of these possible proposals.

CHAPTER 2

ENFORCEMENT OF RIGHTS AND OBLIGATIONS

THE improvement in the mechanism of enforcement of rights and obligations has been hailed as one of the major gains in the Uruguay Round. It is said that it will particularly help the developing countries as the rule-based system which has now emerged will safeguard their interests. Still there are numerous areas in which this mechanism suffers from major deficiencies.

MAIN ELEMENTS OF DISPUTE SETTLEMENT PROCESS

If a country feels that its rights under the WTO Agreements have been adversely affected by the action of another country, or if it feels that another country has not discharged its obligations under the WTO Agreements, it may take recourse to the dispute settlement process of the WTO. First it has to give opportunity to the other country for consultation with a view to resolving the problem. If the problem is not solved, it can approach the Dispute Settlement Body (DSB) of the WTO for formation of a panel which will consider the case.

If such a request is made, the DSB has to form the panel. The refusal is possible only if the DSB decides by consensus not to form the panel. It is nearly impossible, as such a consensus will need the agreement even of the country which has asked for the formation of the panel.

The panel, usually constituted of three or five independent experts, goes into the dispute, considers the points made by the parties to the dispute and gives its findings. The report of the panel has to be adopted by the DSB. Non-adoption is nearly impossible, as it needs the agreement even of the party in whose favour the panel has pronounced its findings.

The country which has been found at fault, has to act in accordance with the recommendations of the panel. If it fails to act in this manner, the affected country can approach the DSB which will permit it to take retaliatory measures against the erring country.

In this process, specific time frames have been fixed for various stages, e.g., for the decision of the DSB to form the panel, finalisation of the terms of reference and the membership of the panel, preparation of the report of the panel, adoption of the report by the DSB, implementation of the recommendations of the panel by the erring country, etc.

IMPROVEMENTS IN THE PROCESS

Earlier, a country against which the complaint has been made might have delayed the process at various stages, particularly at the time of the decision to form the panel and again when the report of the panel would be considered for adoption. These decisions earlier depended on the consensus of all countries present in the meeting where the matter was being considered. Hence on several occasions, the country against which the complaint had been made would delay the process, and sometimes would be able to stop the process altogether. Now it is not possible, as has been explained earlier. The decisions are almost automatic, except if there is a negative consensus, i.e., if the DSB decides by consensus not to form the panel or not to adopt the report, which is almost impossible as it will need the agreement even of the country which gains by the positive decision.

Further, by prescribing the time frames for various stages, undue and deliberate delays have been eliminated.

Thus an aggrieved country has now the confidence that decision on its grievances will be possible within a stipulated time frame and also that the erring party will implement the recommendations within a specified time, or else it will have the possibility of imposing retaliatory measures against the erring country.

All this improvement has brought considerable seriousness into the dispute settlement process. And also there is a degree of confidence that grievances will not be ignored at the instance of powerful countries.

PROBLEMS WITH THE DISPUTE SETTLEMENT PROCESS

No doubt, the process has become more efficient and predictable, but it may still not be quite effective and useful for weak trading partners like the developing countries. It suffers from some basic handicaps and limitations which need attention. Some of these are enumerated below.

(I) Delayed relief

The system permits a delay of more than two years before full corrective action is taken by the erring country. Thus the aggrieved country may have to wait for this long period before it gets full relief. The reasons for the possible delay are explained below.

The process of consultation is a pre-condition for the request for the formation of the panel and it may take two months. Immediately after the request is made for the formation of the panel, the DSB decides to form the panel. Normally the terms of reference of the panel and the membership would get decided without delay. The panel gets six months to issue the final report. If a party to the dispute is not satisfied with the report, it may decide to go in for an appeal. In fact, in most of the important cases, it is likely that the party against whom the panel has given its finding, may prefer to file an appeal. In that case, the matter is referred to the Appellate Body which may take 60 days to give its findings.

After the report of the panel or of the Appellate Body is placed before the DSB, it will normally be adopted without any delay. The erring party has to implement the recommendations immediately; but if immediate compliance is impracticable, the erring party has to indicate a time frame for implementing the recommendations. In case there is no agreement on the time frame, the matter will be referred to arbitration. The guideline to the arbitrator is that the reasonable period to implement the recommendations should not exceed 15 months from the date of adoption of the report by the DSB.

In this manner, nearly 27 months may elapse by the time the harmful action or inaction of the erring country against the complaining country gets fully remedied. It is likely in some cases that this time period gets shortened by quicker action at various stages of the process. In fact, the erring countries have been currently complying with the recommendations promptly. But it is not unreasonable to anticipate that in most of the important and difficult cases, the permissible long time- span of more than two years will be more a reality than an exception. In any case the dispute settlement process does provide for this delay, as has been explained above.

This delay in getting relief may be damaging for the complaining country; and it will be certainly so if the complaining country is a developing country. Developing countries have weak economies and in most cases fragile trade links. The importers in the erring countries are more likely to shift their sources of supply rather than wait for the corrective actions to be completed. The exporters in the complaining countries will thereby lose their exports and export prospects through no fault of theirs or their countries. It will also have an immediate adverse impact on production. These countries have a weak production base, and it may get hurt irreparably in those lines of products which face trade action (later found to be wrong) in important importing countries. Thus, even if the erring country takes corrective steps as a result of a successful dispute settlement process, the relief may come too late for a weak country to be of much practical use.

(II) Illusory relief

For weak countries like developing countries, even this delayed relief may prove to be totally illusory in important cases. The problem lies in the weakness of the mechanism of enforcement of the DSB's decisions. In fact the DSB has no way of enforcing its decisions on the erring country. It is left very much to the good sense of the country concerned. The ultimate weapon is retaliation by the aggrieved country, but it is generally not practicable for a weak country as explained below.

The old GATT system and even the new WTO system depend very much on the moral pressure on the countries concerned for the implementation of the decisions. Generally it has worked well, as the countries concerned have generally decided to abide by the decisions, and taken corrective actions promptly. But the real test of the system comes in hard and important cases where vital interests are involved.

Two recent cases deserve recalling in this regard. In the case of the US against the banana import regime of the European Union, the panel gave its finding that the right of the US was being nullified or impaired by the action of the European Union. When the report of the panel came up before the GATT Council (in those pre-WTO days, the Council used to consider these matters), the EU opposed adoption of the report and it could not be adopted. The EU considered this matter, which was linked to its agreements with the African and Caribbean countries, of vital interest for its member countries and fought hard in the Council. It could stop the adoption of the report in the Council in those days of the old GATT system of dispute settlement. If this case had come up in the WTO, though it could not stop the adoption of the report, it could still decide not to implement the recommendations, if it considered that its banana regime was of vital interest to its member countries. The political embarrassment in non-implementation would in no way be more than what it was in blocking the adoption of the report.

The second case relates to the complaint of Nicaragua against the US. The panel gave its findings against the US and the report was adopted by the Council. But the US still refused to implement the recommendations on the ground that its vital interests were involved.

These two cases have been cited above to indicate that the force of moral pressure in the WTO cannot always be depended upon in real hard cases. And it is in these cases that the interest of the complainant also is vitally involved. Let us examine what the present system provides as relief in such cases.

If the recommendations are not implemented by the erring country, the complaining country can ask the former for compensation; and if there is no settlement, it can request the DSB for authorisation to suspend some concessions or other obligations in respect of the erring country. Normally the DSB has to authorise this. Any decision otherwise is almost impossible as it will need the agreement even of the country requesting such authorisation. After receiving such authority, the complaining country can suspend the concessions or other obligations. Such retaliatory measure must not be more than what is considered equivalent to the nullification or impairment of benefits suffered by the complaining country.

In real hard cases where the erring country decides that it should not implement the recommendations because its vital interests are involved, the only ultimate relief for the complaining country is getting the authorisation to take retaliatory measures.

These measures are generally in the form of additional duty on some products of the erring country or quantitative restrictions on the imports from that country. A country which is not very strong economically, as is the case with almost all developing countries, will find this ultimate solution not very practical, particularly for two reasons.

First, if the erring country is economically and politically strong, any retaliatory action against it is likely to have political and economic implications which a weak country would like to avoid. Second, a retaliatory additional duty or quantitative restriction always involves an economic cost, as the import of goods in question gets more costly in this manner.

Hence in serious disputes between a strong and a weak country, the latter is at a disadvantage in enforcing its right or in ensuring the discharge of the obligations of the former. To that extent the present dispute settlement process may not provide adequate relief.

(III) Constraints on panels in anti-dumping

The cases relating to anti-dumping have been excluded from the purview of normal dispute settlement process. This exceptional provision has been included not in the agreement on Dispute Settlement Understanding, but in the Agreement on Anti-dumping. Severe constraints have been placed on the role of the panels in disputes relating to anti-dumping. Considering that developed countries have lately been using anti-dumping actions as neo-protectionist measures and also that mostly the developing countries are the victims of such actions, the constraints on the panels handling this subject put developing countries at a serious disadvantage. It is useful to explain in detail how the normal process of dispute settlement has been subverted by this provision in the Agreement on Anti-dumping.

In the normal process of dispute settlement, the panels have to make an "objective assessment of the facts of the case and the applicability of and conformity with the relevant covered agreements". Thus the panel has to give a finding whether the action or inaction in question is in conformity with the relevant agreement or whether it violates any provision of the agreement. But in the case of anti-dumping, the relevant provision in the Agreement on Anti-dumping does not permit the panels to determine whether or not the measure under examination is consistent with the agreement. The role of the panel is limited to determining whether the establishment of facts by the domestic authorities of the government taking the measure has been proper and objective and whether the evaluation of the facts has been unbiased and objective. Thus the panels can only examine the process of determination of facts and their evaluation by the domestic authorities. They cannot draw conclusions as to whether or not rights have been violated or obligations have been discharged.

Further, if the relevant provisions of the agreement admit of more than one permissible interpretation, the panel must declare the anti-dumping measure in conformity with the agreement, if it rests upon one of these permissible interpretations. Normally, a government justifies its measures on the basis of its own interpretation of the provisions of some agreement. It is very difficult to argue that the interpretation is not permissible. If there are possibilities of multiple interpretations, the panels generally weigh all of them and give their own preferred interpretation; and then decide whether or not the measure in question is in conformity with the particular provision of the agreement. In examining an anti-dumping measure, the panels have been restrained from following this practice.

If any possible interpretation is to be taken as valid, it will be almost impossible to challenge an action, as it will invariably have the support of the particular interpretation of the government taking the action. And as mentioned above, it will be extremely difficult to argue that the particular interpretation is absurd and not possible.

Some major industrialised countries which have been taking numerous anti-dumping actions against developing countries have succeeded in incorporating this debilitating provision in the Agreement on Anti-dumping, and thereby, they have ensured a certain degree of freedom of action in such cases. Developing countries which are very often the targets of such actions will be the victims.

This exceptional provision does not end with the anti-dumping cases. A decision of the Ministerial Meeting in Marrakesh, which adopted the WTO Agreements, says that this provision is to be reviewed after a period of three years with a view to considering the question whether it is capable of general application. There is thus a possibility of constraining the role of the panels in other areas as well. Here lies the seed of making the dispute settlement process in the WTO totally ineffective.

(IV) Delay by panels or Appellate Body

As mentioned earlier, the dispute settlement process provides disciplines of time-limits for various stages. These disciplines are prescribed for the parties to the dispute and also for the panels and the Appellate Body. If the parties do not follow the discipline, they are likely to suffer, as the panels or the Appellate Body will continue consideration of the case further without waiting for the desired representations from the tardy party. This can act as a deterrent against the parties to the dispute delaying the process at any stage. But there is no remedy against the delay by the panel or the Appellate Body itself.

There is a provision that the panel should give its report within six months and the Appellate Body within two months of the matter being referred to them. But there is no mechanism to enforce these time- limits. The DSB depends on the good sense of the panels and the Appellate Body to adhere to the time frame. They may generally follow it. Systemic weakness, however, does exist inasmuch as there is no provision for ensuring that these bodies keep to the time schedules.

(V) Costly process

The dispute settlement process is often very costly for the developing countries. This is particularly so for two reasons. First, the work of the panels has become intensely technical for some time. The panels have started going into fine points of law in analysing the issues before them. The process of preparation of the case, the presentation before the panels and response to the queries of the panels need a high degree of legal training, experience and expertise. Generally the officials of the developing countries handling the subject of foreign trade in their countries or their diplomats do not have enough background, training and experience to handle all this on their own. Even the legal experts of developing countries do not have enough knowledge and experience of handling cases at the international level. Hence, for an effective preparation of the case and for helping them to make presentations before the panels, developing countries often employ the law firms of developed countries.

Second, very often the preparation of the case needs collection of information in other countries and analysing such information. Developing countries generally do not have their own sources for this purpose. For this reason too, they have to employ law firms and other agencies of developed countries.

And such firms and agencies of developed countries are very costly. The result is that the developing countries which have to take an issue before the DSB or which have to defend themselves against the accusations of others, land up paying huge amounts as fees and other charges. Naturally there is a good deal of hesitation before a decision is taken to raise an issue formally in the DSB. Many developed countries do not face this handicap as they are quite capable of meeting the expenditure.

(VI) Cross-retaliation

In the dispute settlement process there is a provision for cross-retaliation as between different sectors and different agreements. In essence it means that for a perceived lapse in the area of services or intellectual property, there may be retaliation in the goods sector, i.e., a country may in such a situation impose restraints on the import of goods. Similarly, for a perceived lapse in the goods sector, there may be retaliation in the areas of services and intellectual property. For cross-sector retaliation it has to be proved that retaliation in the same sector will not be effective.

This provision is more likely to work against the developing countries. In their case it may be easy to establish that retaliation in the areas of services and intellectual property may not be effective, since it does not have much prospect in these areas. Hence a case can be easily made out that in their cases, retaliation only in the goods sector will be effective, even if there is perceived lapse in services or intellectual property areas. The reverse in the case of developed countries will not be valid, because in their cases, it will be very difficult to prove that retaliation in any of these three areas will be ineffective, since they have good prospects in all these areas. Consequently the provision of cross-retaliation is likely to be used mainly against the developing countries.

POSSIBLE SOLUTIONS

The problems discussed above suggest their own solutions. Some suggestions which are by no means exhaustive are given below.

(i)   There should be a provision for quicker relief, if a country has a grievance against another country in respect of the enforcement of its rights or for ensuring the discharge of obligations by the other country. The first step could be to reduce the time now given to the panels and the Appellate Body. Of course, if they get respectively six months and two months as at present, they can discharge their functions at ease; but the quality of their work need not necessarily suffer if the time allotted to them is nearly halved.

There is a natural tendency for fine legal hair-splitting in the panel process, if more time is available. The parties to the dispute also will work with greater urgency if the time allowed to them for the presentation of the case and for response is shorter.

The panels should also be encouraged to prepare shorter reports. It has been seen lately that the panel reports are quite volumi-nous and cumbersome to read. The purpose of the panel process will not be defeated if the reports are very short and succinct. In fact it will improve the efficiency of the process. It will also encourage the panels to limit themselves to the hard core of the issues involved and not stray unnecessarily into wider areas and deeper legal analysis.

(ii) The time frame for compliance of the recommendations of the panels or the Appellate Body by the erring country should be fixed by the panel in its report; it should not be left to be determined first by the parties concerned and later by the process of arbitration. A lot of delay can be avoided if the panels consider this issue also and give their recommendation. The panels, which have the opportunity of being fully familiar with the case, will be in a good position to judge all aspects of the matter, e.g., the suffering being caused to the affected country, the practical considerations in eliminating the measures by the erring countries, etc.

(iii) There should be a provision for compensation by the erring country to the affected country based on the seriousness of the action or inaction and also on the duration of the measure in question. It should not be enough for the erring country to remove the measures after these have been found to be wrong; rather it should be simultaneously necessary for the erring country to give the compensation as mentioned above. It will safeguard the interests of the affected country to some extent against the delays in the process.

The quantum of compensation should be calculated based on a reasonable assessment of the loss caused to the affected country right from the time when the measures were introduced up to the time when these are to be removed. The compensation may be calculated quickly by an arbitrator, and its recommendation should be binding like the recommendations of the panels. The compensation may be in the form of trade benefits, or even in the form of outright financial payment.

(iv)   If the erring country fails to take the corrective action, the retaliation should not be left to be undertaken solely by the affected country. There should be a joint action by all the countries. Modalities may have to be worked out for this purpose, so that there is a uniform approach in this matter. It should particularly be necessary if the complaining country is a developing country and the erring country is a developed one. An idea of joint action, though in another context, is already there in Article XXV of GATT 1994. It need not be limited to only a "joint decision" by the Members, rather it should be extended to taking "concrete joint action" by them through specific measures against the erring country.

(v)   The restrictions on the role of panels in anti-dumping cases should be totally eliminated and this area should be brought under the normal dispute settlement process.

(vi)   It is not possible to enforce time frames on the panels except through moral pressure and strong suggestions in the DSB. The panel members and the Appellate Body members cannot be penalised for any undue delay caused by them. However, there can be some built-in discouragement of delay. For example, while considering the membership of the panel, the past record of members about respecting time frames should be kept in view.

(vii) It has been mentioned above that the developing countries have to shoulder a very heavy burden of cost in preparations and making presentations because of the intense legalistic nature of the panel's work. However it may not be prudent to discourage the panels in this respect directly. Any such move will have the risk of reducing legal objectivity in the consideration of issues. Nevertheless it will be useful to give an overall guidance to the panels not to function like a court of law, but rather like a group of inter-disciplinary experts, ascertaining facts and examining whether or not rights have been infringed or obligations have been discharged. As mentioned above, the reduction of the time available at the disposal of the panels will itself modulate their work in this connection positively. This is likely to reduce the burden of cost on the parties.

This burden can also be reduced to some extent by the active role of the panels in obtaining the information on their own. The panels can seek information and technical advice from any individual or body. In this regard the panels should be encouraged to obtain the information of relevance to the issues if it is so suggested by the parties to the dispute, particularly the developing countries. This will partly reduce the burden of the developing countries in collecting information which they consider relevant to the issues from their angle.

(viii) If one main party in the dispute is a developing country and another main party is a developed country, there should be a provision that the panel should award some cost to the developing country party if its complaint or defence has been found to be correct and has been upheld by the panels. This cost should be paid by the other main party if it is a developed country. If both the main parties are developing countries or developed countries, there need not be any payment of cost by any party to the other.

(ix) Since the provision of cross-retaliation is heavily weighted only against the developing countries, it is fair to remove this provision altogether.

CHAPTER 3

MARKET ACCESS

IN the areas of market access in WTO Agreements, it is claimed that developed countries have made significant concessions to developing countries. However, a close scrutiny does not find this claim to be justified.

The term "market access" covers a large number of subjects which affect the entry of goods in a country directly. It includes measures like tariff and direct quantitative restrictions on imports. The problems related to market access in some specific sectors like agriculture and textiles will be dealt with later in a separate chapter. Besides, the problems of market access flowing from actions, like safeguards, balance of payment measures, countervailing duty and anti-dumping duty will be discussed in the chapters which follow immediately hereafter. This chapter deals with the issues related to tariff and specific non-tariff measures which have been called "grey area" measures.

TARIFFS

It is within the rights of a country to impose tariff, i.e., customs duty on imports. Tariff is imposed on a product at the time of import. A country publicly announces the rates of tariff on different products so that these are widely known to the exporters and importers. Tariffs naturally make the imported products less competitive compared to the like domestic product, since these charges usually get passed on to the consumers as increase in prices. Thus tariffs affect the importability or the market access of the foreign products and protect the domestic industry. Apart from providing such protection, the tariff has two other functions, viz., (i) it is a source of revenue for the government, and (ii) it helps to ration scarce foreign exchange among various competing imports.

The main role of the tariff in developed countries is to provide protection to the domestic industry. It is not very important as a source of government revenue nor as a tool for allocation of foreign exchange. For developing countries, however, all these roles of the tariff are important. Hence these countries have been keeping their tariffs quite high.

Countries have assumed obligations regarding the tariff levels, earlier in GATT and now in WTO. The obligation is on the highest levels of tariffs on specific products. A country commits that it will not raise the levels beyond these highest levels, which are technically called the "bound" levels. These commitments arise out of negotiations in which various countries agree to lower their tariffs on certain products in return for a reduction of tariffs on other products (of its export interest) by other countries. Lately, in the multilateral trade negotiations (MTNs), countries have agreed to reduce their tariffs across the board, with the objective of generally lowering the tariff levels in international trade globally. These "bound" levels of tariffs of every country get recorded in a schedule and are part of the obligations of the country which it cannot violate except under certain, very specific circumstances. There is a schedule of tariffs for each country where bound tariff levels for different products are recorded.

Right from the inception of GATT in 1947, several rounds of MTNs have taken place, and all of them, except the last two, have been almost wholly concerned with improving market access through the reduction of tariffs. The last two rounds, viz., the Tokyo Round (1973-1979) and the Uruguay Round (1986-1994) of MTNs have been concerned also with other important issues, apart from tariffs.

As a result of the exercise of tariff reduction in these rounds, the tariffs are now very much lower in almost all countries. As the competitiveness of the industries of developed countries improved over time and as there was less need for using tariffs to protect their domestic industry, they went on reducing their tariffs. Now their tariffs on industrial products generally stand at low levels. (The situation in the agriculture sector is, however, very different, as will be explained later in the chapter on sectoral issues.) Most of the developing countries also reduced their tariffs to a great extent, even though tariffs in their case have a multiple role and play an important part in the overall economy.

GREY AREA MEASURES

Apart from tariffs, another type of import restraint is in the form of direct quantitative control and restriction on imports of certain products.

Several developed countries have taken import restraint measures quite frequently without any cover of legality. There has been no specific authorisation for such measures. At the same time these measures have not been conclusively pronounced as violating the disciplines of GATT 1994. In fact these measures have not been formally brought before GATT for legal scrutiny. Hence traditionally these measures of developed countries have been called the grey area measures, signifying that these are neither authorised nor specifically condemned as illegal.

The process of grey area measures started with the industries of developed countries being unable to face the competition from the imports from developing countries. In normal course, these industries would have been wound up. But the governments of these developed countries were pressurised by the industry and labour lobbies in these uncompetitive sectors; and they decided on a softer course of curbing the imports, rather than letting the market forces take their own course.

In such a situation, a clear legal option before these countries was to take protective safeguard action under Article XIX of GATT 1994; but such an action would have to be taken globally against the imports from all countries, including the developed countries. This would have been fraught with some risk, as the other developed countries might have taken retaliatory action.

Hence, the developed countries quietly pressurised the developing exporting countries from time to time to restrict their exports informally. The threat was that their exports would be restrained in any case, even if such restrictive action was against the rules of GATT 1994. Of course, the developing countries could have taken the matter to the dispute settlement mechanism. But the whole process was time consuming and complex and also there was the natural hesitation in annoying major importing countries. Hence, very often the targeted developing countries agreed to this informal arrangement of restricting their export of the particular products to these specific developed countries. The process was ironically called "voluntary export restraint (VER)". Indeed there was nothing voluntary in this process; it was simply an exercise of pressure tactics and threats.

Naturally the products selected for such treatment were those being exported from developing countries in large quantities and which had further potential for fast export growth. This resulted in considerable uncertainty in the industrial sectors in these developing countries, as further investments for expansion of capacity would be considered unsafe. Quite naturally, these grey area measures had a long-term injurious impact on the industry, export and overall economy of these developing countries.

Repeated efforts for eliminating these measures or at least bringing them under some discipline in GATT 1994 failed. Developed countries did not want to let go this easy option which they had acquired for themselves in the most unfair manner. Finally, as a result of the Uruguay Round Agreement on Safeguard, all grey area measures will be eliminated by 1 January 1999, and there is a total ban on introducing such measures in future. This discipline will, no doubt, improve the international trading system and bring more credibility to the system. It will certainly be of benefit to the developing countries as these countries have been the real victims of these measures.

IMPROVEMENTS IN MARKET ACCESS

(I)   Tariffs

As mentioned above, tariffs have been reduced and, to that extent, market access has improved. A lot of publicity has been given to the reduction of tariff by developed countries. It has often been said that these countries have reduced their average tariff on industrial products by nearly 40%. It sounds impressive. Actually their trade-weighted average tariff for industrial products has been committed to be reduced from 6.3% to 3.8%. The percentage reduction is really about 40%. But the actual impact on market access of the reduction of tariff cannot be gauged by the percentage reduction; what is relevant for this purpose is the actual decrease in tariff which in this case is from 6.3% to 3.8%.

Let us see what this reduction means in practice. Suppose the unit price of a product being imported is US$100. With the imposition of customs duty, this product would have been priced at US$106.3, whereas with the reduction of tariff, it will now be priced at US$103.8. Thus the actual benefit of market access is only to the extent that the import will be cheaper now by US$2.5 in a price range of about US$100. This picture does not appear as attractive as the presentation that the tariff has been reduced by 40% by the developed countries.

However, even a small reduction of tariff is welcome, but its importance should be seen in relation to the export prospect that it generates.

(II)   Non-tariff measures

As mentioned above, the elimination of quantitative restrictions called the grey area measures is really significant and it will particularly benefit the developing countries. Equally significant is the commitment not to take such measures in future. What is necessary, however, is that countries must remain vigilant so that protectionist pressures in developed countries do not pressurise their governments once again to take similar measures in future. Also the elimination of the existing measures over the four-year period has to be monitored strictly.

(III) *Principal supplying interest*

When a country wants to raise its tariff beyond the bound level, it has to enter into negotiation with other countries which have either the initial negotiating right or principal supplying interest in that product. Normally these countries would have been major exporters at the time of the binding of the tariff or at the time when a raise in the tariff is proposed. Small suppliers were not given this opportunity. In an Understanding in the WTO Agreements, a provision has been made by which even a small supplying country will have this opportunity of negotiation if its export of that product to a specific market has the highest ratio of its total export of that product. This will specially benefit the developing countries, particularly those that have a high degree of dependence on exports of a particular product to a particular country.

DEFICIENCIES

(I) *High tariffs on certain products*

Even though the average trade-weighted tariff on industrial products in developed countries has been reduced to 3.8%, their tariffs on certain products which are of particular export interest to developing countries still continue to be relatively high. Some examples of high tariff sectors are textiles, clothing, leather products, etc. Thus the average reduction does not give the correct picture regarding the improvement of market access for the products of developing countries. Until tariffs on such products are considerably reduced, the benefits of tariff reduction cannot be availed of fully by the developing countries.

A point is often made that with the new trend of globalisation of production it is not quite rational to describe only certain products such as those listed above as the products of interest to the developing countries. It is pointed out that some of them in fact export even sophisticated industrial products. A very limited number of developing countries do take part in the production and export of diversified industrial goods, but a very large number of them still depend on the traditional items of export. Besides, even in the case of the former, the traditional products may have an important role in the economy.

(II)   Tariff escalation

The term tariff escalation in a country means a higher tariff on higher processed products compared to the lower processed ones in a production chain. For example, in the case of leather, tariff escalation would mean that the lowest rate of tariff is on raw leather, a somewhat higher tariff is imposed on more processed leather, and a still higher one on leather products.

Developed countries have introduced tariff escalation in several product sectors. Though there has been an overall reduction of tariff in developed countries, the structure of tariff is such that the rising scale of tariff with the degree of processing continues to be significant in several product chains. The result is that there is higher effective protection on products with higher processing than those with lower levels of processing. Consequently, the export prospect of higher processed products to these countries is comparatively less. It has a direct impact on the upgradation of industry and exports of developing countries which depend a lot on the export of processed natural products. Their raw materials attract less tariff and their industrial products based on these natural products attract more tariff, with the result that there is relatively more discouragement for the export of their processed products.

Tariff escalation has been identified as one of the significant obstacles to the upgradation of natural resource-based industries in developing countries. Hence there has been considerable attention on eliminating or reducing tariff escalation. On several occasions, pious intentions have been expressed for effective action in this field. But tariff escalation in developed countries still continues.

(III)   Possible loophole in prohibition of grey area measures

A loophole can be detected in the provision for prohibition of future grey area measures. The relevant provision of the Agreement on Safeguard says that a Member of WTO must not "seek, take or maintain any voluntary export restraints, orderly marketing arrangements or any other similar measures on the export or the import side". This firm assertion would seem to prohibit either taking such action or asking another country to take such action. Further, this prohibition is applicable to both exports and imports. Thus a country cannot unilaterally impose restraint on import, nor can it ask any exporting country to curtail its export to this country. Similarly, a country cannot ask an importing country to enter into an arrangement to import a certain minimum quantity from that country.

However, a footnote, while giving illustration of "similar measures" mentioned above, includes export moderation, but leaves out minimum import commitment. Though the list in the footnote is only illustrative, the absence of this measure, when other important measures have been included, may be meaningful. This is particularly so, because the absence of this item from the illustrative list seems to leave out the controversial US request to Japan to agree to a minimum level of imports of cars from the US. Through the absence of this measure in this illustrative list, an attempt may be made in future to suggest that seeking minimum import commitment is not violative of this provision of the Agreement.

IMPROVEMENTS NEEDED

(i)   The tariffs on the products of interest to developing countries should be significantly reduced.

An argument to justify high current tariffs is that several developing countries have gained very much from the lowering of tariffs by developed countries in the past. Even without reciprocity, these low tariffs have been applicable to the exports of developing countries through the provision of non-discrimination in WTO which is popularly known as the most-favoured-

nation (mfn) treatment. Thus it is argued that any further lowering of tariffs on the products of interest to the developing
countries is not called for without developing countries also
entering into commitments for further lowering of their own
tariffs.

But one should remember that developed countries have also
gained not insignificantly by the benefits of low tariffs enjoyed
by the developing countries. The latter have availed of this
opportunity to expand their exports and improve their export
production, which, in turn, has enhanced their import needs and
import capacity. And this has provided a good opportunity to
developed countries to expand their own exports to the developing countries. In fact, in the days of recession in the developed
countries, it is the market in developing countries which has
sustained to a great extent the production and employment in
developed countries.

Hence the enjoyment of the benefits of low tariffs by developing
countries through the mfn treatment is not just a one-way
process. Developed countries should not feel complacent that
enough has been done in the field of tariff and that they no longer
need to lower their tariffs on products of interest to developing
countries. They should take the initiative and reduce their high
tariffs on these products. It will enhance their own prospects for
further exports to these countries as has happened in the past.

(ii)   Tariff escalation should be reduced by the developed countries
with the ultimate objective of eliminating it. This will encourage
developing countries to move to higher levels of processing of
natural products, which, in turn, will provide opportunity to
developed countries to expand their export to these countries
Besides, this action will also enhance the confidence of developing countries in the WTO system, as it will remove a long-felt
handicap suffered by them.

(iii)   The provision relating to the future prohibition of grey area
measures (Article 11.1.b of Agreement on Safeguard) should
clearly prohibit seeking minimum import commitment.

(iv)   It is necessary to ensure that the pressures which brought about grey area measures do not emerge again. One effective way of doing this is to have proper structural adjustment in developed countries so that sectors losing on competitiveness have a smoother way to be competitive or to get wound up. It is desirable that developed countries work out specific programmes of structural adjustment in sectors where there have been persistent pressures for protection in the past. These sectors are well identified. These programmes should be notified to the WTO and an appropriate body in the WTO should review the implementation of these programmes periodically.

CHAPTER 4

CONTINGENCY TRADE MEASURES

TRADE restrictive measures are sometimes taken in response to certain well-defined situations. Here two areas will be discussed, viz., (i) balance of payment measures and (ii) safeguard.

BALANCE OF PAYMENT MEASURES

Countries facing balance of payment (BOP) problems, viz., the problems regarding net inflow of foreign currency or reserves of foreign currency, are authorised to take trade restrictive measures in GATT 1994. Article XII of GATT 1994 contains such provisions which are applicable to all countries, both developed and developing; and Article XVIIIB of GATT 1994 contains the provisions on this subject which are applicable only to developing countries. Developed countries have reached a stage when they do not need to invoke these provisions, and generally they have not been invoking the provisions of Article XII now. Several developing countries have also decided that they will not invoke the provisions of Article XVIIIB. Some of them, however, still continue to use these provisions. Even those that have decided not to use these provisions at present, may have to start using them, if their balance of payment situation becomes very difficult. In fact a few of them did feel the need to use BOP provision and other provisions of Article XVIII some time ago, but their proposals were not viewed with favour in the WTO.

MAIN PROVISIONS OF ARTICLE XVIIIB

A developing country with a weak economy and in an early stage of development and also facing balance of payment problems can take price-based measures, like raising tariffs beyond bound levels and it can also impose direct quantitative restrictions on imports. There is a strong guidance in the Uruguay Round Understanding on this subject that quantitative restrictions can be imposed only if it can be shown that price-based measures cannot deal with the BOP problem.

Such measures must not be excessive and should be commensurate with the BOP problem. Further, these measures cannot be taken for protecting the domestic industry.

The measures must be progressively relaxed as the BOP conditions improve and must be totally eliminated when conditions no longer justify their existence.

The use of BOP measures is strictly monitored in the WTO. A country applying BOP measures has to consult with the BOP Committee of the WTO regularly. Such consultation involves a close scrutiny of its policy by other countries, particularly the developed countries. Recent experiences of developing countries facing such consultation show that they have been severely questioned in the committee particularly by the representatives of developed countries, who try to prove that the BOP measures are no longer necessary and these should be terminated. It is getting more difficult for developing countries to take new measures and to defend the measures already taken and continuing.

Most of the developing countries have weak economies and they also face an unpredictable international trading environment; hence it is difficult for them to feel confident about their BOP situation on a long-term basis. And yet several among them have "disinvoked" Article XVIIIB, which means that they have made a formal announcement in the WTO that they would not be resorting to this provision. For some of them it has proved to be problematic, as, soon thereafter, they felt the need for introducing BOP measures, which was strongly opposed by the developed countries. Consequently they found it difficult to re-introduce BOP measures.

PROBLEMS WITH CURRENT PROVISIONS

(I)   Constraints on quantitative restrictions

As mentioned above, constraints have been put on the use of quantitative restrictions such as BOP measures, since it has to be first shown that tariff-type measures will not be adequate to tide over the BOP problem. One important difference between the two types of measures is that direct quantitative restrictions control the imports immediately, whereas the tariff-type measures are not so efficient. In the latter case, the price impact takes time to have its effect on the flow of imports. Besides, the foreign producers and exporters may try to absorb the raised tariff for some time and in that situation the increase in tariff will not result in reduction of imports. Since a country facing BOP problems needs to control imports immediately, the direct quantitative restrictions are certainly more effective and efficient. In that context it does not appear reasonable to restrict the options of the developing countries regarding the measures to be taken. They should be free to choose the measures for controlling the imports as was originally envisaged in Article XVIIIB of GATT 1994.

The restrictions first came in 1979 at the end of the Tokyo Round when it was laid down that priority would be given to the measures having less trade-distorting effect. Now in the Uruguay Round Understanding, further specificity and rigidity have been introduced by the stipulation that countries applying quantitative restrictions must provide justification as to the reasons why price-based measures are not an adequate instrument to deal with the BOP situation.

It has to be noted that there is no such specific constraint in respect of safeguard measures (to be discussed later), which are taken by countries to protect their domestic industries against imports.

(II)   Criteria for BOP problems

No definite criteria have been laid down in respect of the flow of foreign exchange or the reserve of foreign exchange which would enable a country to take BOP measures. For the discussion in the BOP Committee in the WTO, the International Monetary Fund prepares a report which gives information on the economy of the country including its foreign exchange position. The Committee takes a view on the BOP situation of the country based on this information and other relevant information which the country provides. Generally the current foreign exchange reserve and the net inflow of foreign exchange influence the opinion in the Committee.

Many times the problem arises because of the uncertainty of the inflow and reserve of the foreign exchange. For example, in many countries the investors from outside take to portfolio investment, i.e., they invest in short-term deposits and the share-market. In such cases, even though the flow of funds and reserves may be high, there is no stability and certainty as the investors may withdraw their funds sometimes suddenly. In fact it may be difficult for the country to take decisions based on such funds. If such uncertain features of the foreign exchange flow and reserves are not taken into account while considering the BOP situation of the country, it will be seriously prejudiced in respect of its eligibility to take BOP measures.

(III)   Public announcement for elimination of measures

The Uruguay Round Understanding on BOP makes it obligatory for the developing countries that have taken BOP measures to make a public announcement of the time schedules for the elimination of these measures. And reasons with justification have to be given if such public announcement is not possible. Of course, the call for elimination of measures when these are no longer necessary is justified, but the requirement of a public announcement for this purpose appears somewhat misplaced. There is no such requirement placed on developed countries about their grey area measures (discussed earlier). The only requirement in that case is that the countries would notify these measures to WTO by the beginning of March 1995, eliminate these measures by the beginning of 1999 and give to WTO by the end of June 1995, a programme for elimination. There is no mention of any "public announcement" as such. By no stretch of imagination can the BOP measures be said to be more undesirable than the grey area measures. Clearly, the call for public announcement is the result of overenthusiasm on the part of those countries that do not like developing countries to take such measures.

IMPROVEMENTS REQUIRED

(i)   Considering the objectives for which BOP measures have been authorised in Article XVIIIB of GATT 1994, it is desirable to restore to the countries taking such action, the flexibility regarding the type of action to be taken. The countries should be free to take either price-based measures or direct quantitative restrictions as is clearly envisaged in the original Article XVIIIB. There is a system of very strict scrutiny of the BOP problems and BOP measures during the consultations in the BOP Committee. Hence any wrong use of flexibility can always be challenged and examined. To that extent there is already a safeguard against any misuse.

(ii)   While considering the existence of BOP problems in a country, the BOP Committee should take into account the nature and the structural composition of the flow of funds and the reserves. Flows and reserves which, by their nature, are uncertain and unpredictable, should not be taken as evidence of good BOP position. The consideration of stability of the BOP situation is important.

(iii)   The time for making public announcement of the programme of elimination of BOP measures is over. Hence, even though this requirement appears unreasonable as mentioned above, nothing can be done now. However, if some countries have not made any public announcement so far, there should not be any insistence on it.

SAFEGUARD MEASURES

If a product sector of the domestic industry of a country suffers injury from imports, measures for safeguarding that sector can be taken by that country. Such measures can also be taken if there is even a threat of injury. Safeguard measures may be either in the form of raised tariffs (raising the tariff above the bound levels) or in the form of quantitative restrictions on imports.

MAIN ELEMENTS

Specific disciplines have been laid down for taking safeguard action. Certain pre-conditions must be fulfilled. Besides, there are limitations regarding the duration of the action and repetition of the safeguard action. Specific procedure has been laid down for determining the existence of the pre-conditions and imposition of safeguard measures.

A country proposing to take safeguard action has to designate an authority in the country for examination of requests for safeguard action. When such a request is made, the authority will hold an investigation to determine whether (i) there has been an increase in the import in either absolute or relative terms, (ii) the particular sector of the industry has been injured or there is a threat of injury to it, and (iii) the injury or the threat has been caused by the increased import. If the industry has suffered due to some other reasons as well, the import will not be considered as the sole reason for the injury; and in that case safeguard action cannot be taken.

Investigation by the authority has to be open to interested parties and they will be given proper notice for this purpose. The applicants try to prove during the investigation that the imports are causing injury to the domestic industry or threatening to cause it. The defend-ants, i.e., the main exporting countries, try to contest it. One important point to note is that during the investigation, evidence can also be produced to show whether or not the application of safeguard meas-ure would be in the public interest. It means that not only the effects on the domestic producers, importers and exporters are to be considered, but also the impact of the proposed safeguard measure on the public as a whole is to be considered. For example, heavy imports may reduce the price, which would benefit the users. Hence imports may be adverse to the interest of domestic producers, but these may be favourable to the consumers or the user industries. In assessing public interest, all these aspects will have to be taken into consideration.

The authority will consider all aspects and give its findings. Based on the report of the authority, the government may decide to impose safeguard measures.

The Agreement on Safeguard provides for disciplines on the duration of a safeguard measure, progressive liberalisation of the measure and repeated application of a measure.

An important feature of the safeguard measure is that it cannot be targeted at a particular country; it has to be taken against the import from all sources. For example, if tariff is to be raised above the bound levels, the increased tariff will be applicable to all imports, whatever may be the source. If quantitative restrictions have to be imposed, these too have to be directed against imports from all sources. In this case the modality is that the country taking safeguard measure fixes a global quota for the import of that product; and this global quota is allocated by it to the exporting countries. Usually the allocation of the quota is based on the import from the particular country in the previous three years. But the Agreement authorises departure from this norm in certain circumstances. This departure is popularly called the quota modulation. For departure from the norm, a country has to demonstrate that the imports from some countries have increased in disproportionate percentage in relation to the total increase in the import of that product.

This Agreement has prohibited the taking of grey area measures and has prescribed eliminating the existing measures within a time frame as has been explained in the chapter on market access.

There is a *de minimis* provision for developing countries. No safeguard action will be taken against a product of a developing country as long as its share of imports of that product in that importing country does not exceed 3%.

IMPROVEMENTS IN THE SAFEGUARD PROCESS

The description given above would indicate that several improvements have been brought about in the safeguard process in the WTO Agreements. Some of the important ones are listed below.

(i)   The procedure for taking safeguard action has been well codified. It has curtailed subjective actions and judgements; and it has also made the process more enforceable through the dispute settlement mechanism.

(ii)   For a safeguard action, it is necessary to demonstrate the causal link between the import and injury. Thus industries cannot now pressurise governments to take safeguard action merely because they are facing an adverse situation and are in a declining phase.

(iii)   There is a definite time-limit for the measures and specific constraint on repeating the measure.

(iv)   Developing countries are covered by the protection of a 3% *de minimis* limit, as explained above.

PROBLEMS IN THE SAFEGUARD PROCESS

(I)   Risks in quota modulation

As mentioned above, a country imposing quantitative restrictions as a safeguard measure can depart from the normal process of allocation of quota among the exporting countries. There are two uncertainties in this process, viz., first, the criteria which will enable a country to depart from the normal process have not been spelt out clearly. The only substantive guideline is that imports from some countries should have increased in disproportionate percentage to the total increase in the import. What would constitute "disproportionate" is not specified. What would be the period of consideration is also not clear. Other relevant factors like low base of import from some countries, decline of the relevant production sector in some other countries, etc. have not been mentioned as guiding factors. This may introduce an element of unfairness in this whole process, with particular risks to developing countries trying to expand their production and export from a low base. For example, even if a developing country has gained a relatively high share of the "increase in the imports", it still may not be having a comparatively high share of the import of that product in that country because of its earlier low share.

Second, the permissible extent of departure from the norm of allocation of the quota has also not been specified. This can give unduly unfettered discretion to the country to fix low quotas for the countries which qualify for the quota modulation.

(II)   De minimis *provision*

Though there is a *de minimis* provision for developing countries in the Agreement, as mentioned earlier, it is not clear how it will operate. For example, in tariff-type safeguard measures, it is not clear whether the higher tariff will not be applicable to developing countries, covered by the *de minimis* clause. Similarly, in case of quantitative restrictions on quota, it is not quite clear if these developing countries will be totally free from any restraint. A simple reading of the relevant provisions of the Agreement does indicate that this would be actually the case; but considering the past practices which were prejudicial to developing countries, there may be a genuine fear that lack of an explicit provision may encourage countries imposing safeguard measures to miss this point.

(III)   *Details in procedure*

The procedural details for taking safeguard measures have been very well laid down. As indicated above, this will bring in considerable objectivity to the system. But another aspect is that it puts great demands also on developing countries which propose to take safeguard measures. Normally this should not be resented; but the situation at present is that several developing countries that have recently liberalised their import regime may not have enough experience of conducting investigations and following other mandatory procedures. The risk is that even though the action may be justified on merits, it may still be technically pronounced incorrect, because certain fine points of procedure have not been meticulously followed.

SUGGESTIONS TO OVERCOME THESE PROBLEMS

(i)   Criteria for selecting countries for allocation of quota-share lower than the norm should be strengthened. Along with the share of the increase in import, the share in the actual import should also be an important criterion. Besides, it should also be relevant to consider whether or not such increased shares have features of stability.

(ii)   Clear limits should be fixed for the extent of departure from the norms in allocation of the quota-share. The objective should be to reduce the scope of subjective decision by the country taking the safeguard action.

(iii) Since developing countries have often been the victims of unilateral actions, there is a natural apprehension that the provision of the modulation of quota may unfairly make them the targets. It is therefore necessary to have very strict monitoring of the implementation of this provision. An effective monitoring in the Committee on Safeguard and the Council for Trade in Goods may allay the fears of developing countries to some extent.

(iv)   It should be clearly spelt out in the decisions of the Committee on Safeguard that developing countries falling within the *de minimis* limit will be excluded from the scope of the safeguard measure, even though the particular measure is applicable to developed countries and other developing countries.

       Further, if a developing country comes out of the *de minimis* limit, the measure should not be imposed on it immediately. It should be subject to the measure only if it continues to be out of the *de minimis* limit for a specified minimum period, say, two years.

(v) There should be a formal decision in the Committee on Safeguard that procedural deficiencies of developing countries in course of imposition of safeguard measures will be overlooked, if the deficiencies are of technical nature and do not substantively vitiate the process.

CHAPTER 5

Measures Against Unfair Trade Practices

TRADE gets adversely affected by unfair trade practices, like inadmissible subsidies and dumping. Such practices lower the prices artificially and constrict the competitive position of other like products which are not subsidised or dumped. Elaborate rules have been made in the Uruguay Round Agreements for taking action against such practices. There has been considerable improvement in this process, and yet there are areas which need further attention for improvement. Here two subjects will be separately discussed, viz., (i) subsidies and countervailing measures and (ii) anti-dumping.

SUBSIDIES AND COUNTERVAILING MEASURES

Sometimes governments provide subsidy to their industry and export through direct financial contribution or waiving of some payments. It enhances the competitive position of the industry and trade; and under certain circumstances, it may provide unfair advantage to them *vis-à-vis* the industry and trade of another country. Hence disciplines have been laid down in the WTO Agreements on the grant of subsidies and also on taking action against the subsidies given by other countries.

MAIN ELEMENTS OF THE DISCIPLINE

Types of subsidy

Subsidies are of two broad types based on the target beneficiary, viz., (i) domestic subsidy or production subsidy which is given to the domestic industry in the process of production and (ii) export subsidy, i.e., the subsidy given in the process of export, generally to the exporters.

The export subsidy directly enhances the competitive position of the exporter *vis-à-vis* the exporters of other countries or domestic suppliers. The production subsidy enhances the competitive position by providing support at the stage of production.

Based on permissiveness, there are three classes of subsidy, viz., (i) prohibited subsidy, (ii) permissible subsidy and (iii) actionable subsidy. The third category is such where the subsidy is permissible up to a certain extent, and beyond that, the subsidy will be subject to counteraction by affected countries.

Two types of subsidies are prohibited, viz., (i) export subsidy, i.e., the subsidy which is contingent on export, and (ii) import substitution subsidy, i.e., subsidy provided to the domestic industry for using domestic raw materials or intermediate products in preference to imported products.

Two types of subsidies are permissible, viz., (i) non-specific subsidy, i.e., those subsidies which are not specific to particular industrial units or industrial sectors, but are generally applicable to all sectors, e.g., subsidies provided to small-scale industries in general, and (ii) subsidies which are specific but meant for research or development of disadvantaged regions or environmental purposes.

Subsidies which are neither prohibited nor permitted can also be given, provided they do not harm the industry and export of some other country. If harm is caused by this third category of subsidy, the country which is adversely affected can take action against this subsidy.

Action against subsidy

If a country gives prohibited subsidy, any other country affected by it can take two alternative types of actions against it, viz., (i) it can take recourse to the dispute settlement process for having the subsidy eliminated, or (ii) it can impose countervailing duty on the subsidised product after following the prescribed process, in case its domestic industry suffers injury or is threatened with injury because of the subsidised export. If there is no such injury, the route of the countervailing duty is not available.

If a country gives actionable subsidy, again two alternative types of action by the affected country can be possible against it, as described briefly below:

(i)   If injury is being caused or threatened by the subsidised product, countervailing duty can be imposed on it, following the specified procedure.

(ii)   If there is injury, threat of injury, nullification or impairment of benefits under GATT 1994 or serious prejudice, the affected country can take recourse to the dispute settlement process for elimination of the subsidy.

Serious prejudice to a country has been clearly defined for this purpose in the Agreement. It includes adverse effect on (i) its domestic production, or (ii) its export to the subsidising country, or (iii) its export to a third country.

Action can also be taken against permissible subsidy if an affected country finds that there is a serious adverse effect on its domestic industry. The affected country can take it up in the Committee on Subsidy. The possible relief is that either the subsidy is eliminated or the affected country is permitted to take some appropriate countermeasure against the subsidising country.

Investigation for countervailing duty

Detailed procedure has been laid down for investigation about the existence of subsidy, injury and causal link between the subsidy and injury. The procedure is lengthy and tedious, but it ensures a certain degree of objectivity and transparency in the process. Also it helps to resort to the dispute settlement process in case the procedure has not been properly followed. The countervailing duty can be imposed only if it is established that subsidy and injury or its threat exist and the injury or the threat is being caused by the subsidised import.

Special provisions for developing countries

Before the WTO Agreements came into effect, developing countries had wide flexibility in the area of subsidies. In fact, subsidy was well recognised as an important tool for the development of developing countries. These countries were using subsidies to diversify and develop their production and export. It was considered necessary as their production and trade suffered from severe handicaps, and it would be difficult for them to compete in the world market. Most of these handicaps continue even now; but the Uruguay Round Agreement on Subsidies has severely curtailed their discretion to use subsidy.

The industry and trade in developed countries have a distinct advantage over their counterparts in developing countries because of three basic factors, viz., (i) adequate capital available at comparatively low cost, (ii) easy availability of high technology, and (iii) highly developed infrastructure. Most of the developing countries cannot aspire to attain these healthy attributes in the foreseeable future. Hence the need arises for government support of the industry and trade so that they can overcome some of the handicaps. This basic fact does not seem to have weighed much in the Uruguay Round.

However, the Agreement on Subsidy does contain some special provisions for developing countries. The least developed countries and other developing countries with the GNP per capita less than US$1,000 per annum are exempt from the prohibition of export subsidy, until they reach the level of export competitiveness (defined as the stage when the export of the particular product of the country reaches a level of 3.25% of the world export of that product). Other developing countries can continue with the export subsidy until 1 January 2003.

The prohibition on the import-substitution subsidy will not apply to the least developed countries until 1 January 2003, and to other developing countries until 1 January 2000.

In respect of actionable subsidy, there is a presumption of the existence of serious prejudice under certain situations, e.g., when the subsidy exceeds 5% or when it is given to cover operating losses of an industry, etc. In the case of developing countries there is no such presumption. It means that in their cases the affected countries will have to prove the existence of serious prejudice based on positive evidence.

There is a *de minimis* provision that no countervailing duty will be imposed on the product of a least developed country or another developing country with per capita GNP less than US$1,000 per annum, if the subsidy on the product does not exceed 3% of its value. This limit is 2% for other developing countries. There is also a *de minimis* level for the volume of the subsidised import from a developing country, which is 4% of the total import of the product in the affected country.

Then there are some minor special provisions regarding limitations on taking countermeasures against developing countries.

IMPROVEMENTS IN THE SYSTEM

(I) Objective procedure

As mentioned above, detailed procedure has been laid down for taking action against subsidies, particularly for imposing countervailing duty. It has brought in considerable objectivity in the system. The process has also been made transparent.

(II) Linkage between injury and subsidy

Before imposing countervailing duty, it has to be established that injury has been caused or is threatened by the subsidised import. The need of establishing such clear linkage will reduce the possibility of imposing the duty under undue pressure from the domestic industry lobby.

(III) De minimis *provision*

The *de minimis* provision of exclusion of developing countries from the countervailing duty up to a certain degree of subsidy and subsidised import is helpful for small suppliers and moderate subsidisers.

IMPORTANT DEFICIENCIES

(I) *Subsidies in developing countries*

The types of subsidies which are commonly used in developed countries have been included in the non-actionable category, whereas those which are needed in developing countries have been left out of this special dispensation. The former types of subsidies are those for research, regional development and environmental protection. But the subsidies which are generally used by developing countries for their industrialisation and development have not been made non-actionable. In this category one can enumerate measures such as cheaper provision of finance for investment and working capital, financial support for absorption and adaptation of new and advanced technology, subsidy for diversification of market, help in market development etc. As mentioned above, such subsidy practices were earlier considered as recognised instruments for development. And the Uruguay Round Agreement on Subsidies either prohibits them or makes them actionable, whereas the common subsidy practices of the developed countries enumerated above have been put into the non-actionable category.

(II) *Dispute settlement process*

As mentioned earlier, the dispute settlement process has become very complex and technical. A developing country, while filing a complaint about the subsidy of another country, has to collect and analyse a lot of information on the subsidy practice of that country. Likewise, when it is defending itself against the complaint of another country, it may have to collect information bearing on the existence of injury to the industry in that country and the causal linkage between its export and the injury. Often collection of such information is a very difficult and costly task. This puts the developing countries in a position of disadvantage, in spite of all the helpful features of the dispute settlement process in the area of subsidy.

(III) Countries with low GNP per capita

As mentioned above, developing countries with GNP per capita less than US$1,000 per annum have certain special dispensation in respect of subsidies. A list of such countries has been given in an Annex to the Agreement. A practice has developed that as any of these countries reaches this limit of income, it is immediately removed from this list. In some cases the rise in income may be a temporary phenomenon and not a structural feature. In that situation it will be inappropriate to remove the country from the Annex. It is desirable to take into account whether the rise in income has some degree of stability.

(IV) Competitiveness

A developing country is excluded from some facilities regarding subsidies on a product in respect of which its export share in the world trade reaches 3.25% or more in two consecutive years. The exclusion is automatic once this stage is reached. However, there is no explicit provision for automatic inclusion if the export share later falls below this level.

NECESSARY IMPROVEMENTS

(i)   Subsidies on domestic production and export in developing countries necessary for their industrialisation and development should be categorised as non-actionable.

(ii)   Panels should exercise their power to collect with their own efforts the information considered relevant for the case of the developing country party to a dispute. There should also be a provision for the WTO Secretariat to collect the information indicated by the developing country party as relevant to its case. These provisions are particularly important in the areas of subsidy and anti-dumping where very detailed factual information is often necessary and relevant.

(iii)   A developing country should be excluded from Annex VII to the Agreement on Subsidy only when its GNP per capita remains at the critical level of US$1,000 per annum on a stable basis for two years.

(iv)   When the export share of a developing country in respect of a product falls below 3.25%, it should automatically be eligible for the benefits allowed to the countries having less than this critical share of export.

ANTI-DUMPING

Dumping commonly means exporting a product at very low prices. Technically, a product is said to be dumped by the exporter, if its export price is lower than the price at which a like product is sold in the exporting country. Dumping is considered an unfair trade practice, as it adversely affects the normal competition. Dumping is sometimes used as a predatory practice to eliminate competition. The Uruguay Round Agreement on Anti-dumping is a very detailed agreement and also very complex as it tries to adopt the anti-dumping practices followed by major developed countries.

MAIN ELEMENTS

The relief against dumping is the anti-dumping duty on the dumped import to offset the effect of dumping in the market. Anti-dumping duty can be imposed by a country only after following a specific procedure prescribed in the Agreement on Anti-dumping. The process of anti-dumping action usually starts with an application by the domestic industry to the government for taking such action. The allegations made in the application are examined by the competent authority (established by the government for such purpose) in an investigation where all interested parties are given an opportunity to present their cases. In the course of the investigation, the competent authority has to determine (i) the existence of dumping, and if it exists, the margin of dumping, (ii) the existence of injury and (iii) the existence of a causal relationship between the dumped import and injury. It is very similar to the case of the investigation on subsidy.

The Agreement gives in great detail how the existence of dumping and the margin of dumping will be determined. The margin of dumping is the difference between the export price and the normal value. Generally the normal value is the price at which a like product is sold in the domestic market. If this price cannot be reliably determined, there are alternative ways of calculating it. One very common way is to calculate the cost of production and add to it the administrative, selling and general expenses and profit. All these calculations are extremely complex, as these try to assimilate the procedures followed for some time by the major developed countries.

Based on the report of the competent authority, the government decides on the imposition of the anti-dumping duty. The duty cannot be higher than the dumping margin.

It is relevant to draw a distinction between subsidy and dumping. The former is the action of a government, while the latter is the action of firms. Thus in the investigation on subsidy, the government that is alleged to give subsidy is the defendant, whereas in the investigation on dumping, the firms alleged to be dumping their products are the defendants.

The authority has the obligation to determine the individual margin of dumping in the case of each known exporter or producer of the product under investigation. If the numbers are large so as to make the individual determination impractical, the examination may be limited to a reasonable number of parties using statistically valid samples.

There is a *de minimis* provision applicable to all countries, whether developed or developing. No anti-dumping action will be taken if the dumping margin is less than 2% of the export price. Similarly, no anti-dumping action against the product of a country will be taken, if the volume of the dumped import is less than 3% of the total import of like products in the affected importing country.

IMPROVEMENTS IN THE SYSTEM

(i)   In the process of the implementation of the Anti-dumping Code of the Tokyo Round, various major developed countries evolved their own systems of determining the dumping margin. This increased the scope of subjectivity and also created serious uncertainty in the process. The Uruguay Round Agreement on Anti-dumping gives detailed specific methods for calculating the export price, the normal value and for comparing the two to determine the existence and margin of dumping. This has brought in considerable objectivity and predictability in this process.

(ii)   As in the case of subsidy, the clear criterion of causal linkage between the dumping and injury reduces the incidence of imposition of anti-dumping duty merely on the pressure of the domestic industry.

DEFICIENCY IN THE SYSTEM

(I) *Constraints on the role of panels*

The most serious deficiency in the anti-dumping process is the exclusion of this area from the normal dispute settlement process as has been explained in detail in the chapter on enforcement of rights and obligations. The role of the panels has been curtailed. They are not required to determine whether any measure of a country relating to this area violates the provisions of the Agreement; their role is limited to examining whether the facts have been determined properly and whether the evaluation of the facts has been done in an unbiased and objective manner. Further the interpretation of the country taking a measure will not be challenged if there is a possibility of multiple interpretations, even if the panel does not agree with that interpretation. Clearly, the dispute settlement process has been made very weak in the area of anti-dumping.

(II) *Complexity of the process*

The Agreement is very complex, in fact even more complex than the Agreement on Subsidies. And developing countries are at a disadvantage because of the complexity. Developing countries often find it difficult to collect relevant factual information relating to the normal value and the export price. The trade and industry of the developing countries and even the government machinery are not well equipped to locate the sources of such information in other countries and to collect them. As mentioned in the chapter on the enforcement of rights and obligations, very often the services of the law firms of developed countries have to be utilised which naturally proves very costly for the developing countries.

Considering the vast differences in the resources at the disposal of developed countries and developing countries, the process of anti-dumping enquiries gets very much tilted against the developing countries which suffer from this handicap both as complainants and defendants. The handicap can be reduced to some extent only if they are prepared to spend enormous amounts in hiring the services of the law firms of developed countries. In fact even to get the normal protection of this multilateral agreement, they hesitate to initiate the process because of the expenditure involved.

NECESSARY IMPROVEMENTS

(i)   The constraint on the panels should be eliminated and anti-dumping should be brought within the folds of normal dispute settlement process.

(ii) Measures for making the process less costly as mentioned in the section on subsidies are applicable here too with greater relevance.

CHAPTER 6

AGREEMENTS IN SPECIFIC SECTORS

THE two main sectoral agreements in the Uruguay Round Agreements are those in the sectors of agriculture and textiles. There are three other sectoral agreements, viz., those relating to civil aircraft, bovine meat and dairy products; but these are plurilateral agreements (as against the other agreements which are multilateral agreements) and are applicable to only a limited number of countries that have accepted them. The agreements in the sectors of agriculture and textiles, on the other hand, are like any other general agreements of the Uruguay Round which are applicable to all Members of WTO. Here a brief description and analysis of the agreements in the sectors of agriculture and textiles will be given separately.

AGRICULTURE

Agriculture was under a soft discipline in GATT compared to the industrial products. The Uruguay Round Agreement on Agriculture brings this sector under tighter discipline. In many ways it is still a soft discipline compared to that applied to the industrial sector, though in some ways the disciplines in this field have been made more stringent.

MAIN ELEMENTS OF THE AGREEMENT

The commitments in this sector extend over three areas, viz., (i) market access, i.e., disciplines on import restraint, (ii) domestic support, i.e., government support to domestic producers, and (iii) export subsidy, i.e., government support for export.

The commitments of different countries are inscribed in the country schedules which are integral parts of the Agreement. All these schedules of different countries are kept together in bound volumes. One has to consult them to know the commitments made by any particular country in the three areas mentioned above.

These commitments of various countries were arrived at in negotiations among them before the end of the Uruguay Round; and these were submitted by the respective countries to the WTO Secretariat for inclusion in the schedule. These commitments are supposed to be based on an agreed set of modalities which were contained in a modality paper which does not form part of the Agreement now; it only served the purpose of forming a basis for the calculation of commitments of different countries.

The modality paper first gave the guidelines for the calculation of the base levels of import restraint, domestic support and export subsidy. Then it laid down the mandatory percentage reductions in these figures to be achieved over the implementation period. Countries were expected to follow the modality paper in calculations of the respective base levels and also in calculating the final reduced levels at the end of the implementation period. Then annual levels were calculated based on simple distribution of the target reduction over the implementation period. These have been included in the country schedules without mentioning the basis of calculations and without referring to the modality paper.

The schedule prepared by a country was expected to be verified by other countries; but the time was too short for any thorough verification. Some detailed studies have indicated that in several cases, the modalities were not strictly observed.

Market access

An important step in the market access is what has been termed as "tariffication", i.e., conversion of non-tariff measures into tariff equivalents, which added to the ordinary tariff, make the totality of the market restraint. All countries have to tariffy their non-tariff import restraint measures, like total import ban, quantitative restrictions on import, etc. None of these measures can normally continue now under the Agreement. The only exceptions are measures taken under specific provisions of GATT 1994, like BOP measures and safeguard measures. Besides, four Members, viz., Japan, Republic of Korea, Philippines and Israel, have taken the alternative route of retaining the measures for some products and allowing a minimum market access opportunity for those products. After tariffication, all countries have to bind their tariffs on all agricultural items, the level of tariffs starting from the initial bound levels in 1995 going down to the final reduced levels at the end of the implementation period (the year 2000 for developed countries and 2004 for developing countries).

In several cases, particularly in the case of some developed countries, the resultant total tariff is exceedingly high. Some of these typically high tariffs are

US: sugar (244.4), peanuts (173.8), milk (82.6);
EU: beef (213), wheat (167.7), sheep meat (144);
Japan: wheat product (388.1), wheat (352.7),
            barley products (361);
Canada: butter (360), cheese (289), eggs (236.3).

Quite clearly these are prohibitive tariffs. These have been calculated by taking very high tariff equivalents of the non-tariff measures.

Various countries have, however, prescribed imports up to a limited extent on much lower tariffs. This is described later in the section on tariff quotas.

As mentioned earlier, the BOP measures taken by developing countries are not covered by the process of tariffication. In fact several developing countries taking BOP measures have not considered them for tariffication. The implication is that they will not be able to take advantage of the tariff equivalents of these measures, when they lose the cover of the BOP provision of Article XVIIIB of GATT 1994. At that time they will have to eliminate these measures and continue only with the ordinary tariff.

Domestic support

Domestic subsidy for each country has been quantified, and the country has committed to limit the subsidy up to a particular level in 1995. Thereafter, the subsidy is reduced in each year of the implementation period, and the ceiling of subsidy in each of these years is recorded in the schedule of the country. An important point to note is that the commitment is in respect of the overall quantum of support in terms of the annual amounts. There is no separate limit for subsidy on any product, nor is there any ceiling on the rates of subsidy. A country is free to choose the products and the rates of subsidy within the overall limit of the total amount of subsidy during that year. For other trading partners, it creates a considerable degree of uncertainty, as they may not know beforehand the competitiveness of various agricultural products in that country.

If a country has not mentioned in its schedule the levels of subsidies applicable in different years, it cannot apply any subsidy in the agriculture sector beyond the *de minimis* levels.

There are some exemptions for developing countries from the disciplines of domestic support. The items of exemption cover investment subsidies, input subsidies generally available to low-income and resource-poor producers and support to producers to give up growing illicit narcotic crops.

There is a general *de minimis* exclusion of product-specific subsidy from the discipline, if it does not exceed 5% of the value of production of that product. In the case of non-product-specific subsidies, the *de minimis* level is 5% of the value of total agricultural production. Both these *de minimis* levels for developing countries are 10%.

Certain other types of measures are also exempt from the commitment of reduction, e.g., general services, like research, pest and disease control etc., stock holding for food security, domestic food aid, relief against natural disasters, assistance for curtailing production in various ways, etc. For developing countries, the purchase and sale of government stock at administered prices and also the provision of food to the poor at subsidised and reasonable prices are exempt from the reduction commitment. The subsidy involved in the purchase of government stock, however, is to be included in the calculation of the level of annual subsidy, which, in turn, is subject to annual ceilings. This means that the ceiling reduction from year to year has to be carried out by reducing other types of subsidies, if this particular item is not subject to reduction. This will be possible anyway, even without this special dispensation.

Export subsidy

The commitment on export subsidy by the countries is on two items, viz., (i) the total budgetary outlays and (ii) the total quantity of export covered by export subsidy. For each year of the implementation period, these two figures are noted in the country schedule. If a country has not mentioned in its schedule any figures for the export subsidy, it will not be able to provide export subsidy in the agriculture sector.

Developing countries are exempt from the disciplines on two types of export subsidy, viz., (i) payment to reduce the cost of marketing, including handling, upgrading, processing and international transport and freight, and (ii) provision of internal transport and freight for export shipment on terms more favourable than that for domestic shipments.

Developing countries

There is no obligation on the least developed countries regarding reduction of tariff, domestic support and export subsidy. However, even these countries have to bind tariffs on all agricultural items.

For the other developing countries, the modality paper contained a lower percentage reduction and longer implementation period.

There was a Ministerial Decision at Marrakesh for the special problems of the net food importing developing countries. The decision is to work towards more effective food aid. Further, the special difficulties faced by these countries in importing foodstuff have been recognised. However, there is no decision about any specific action in this regard.

MAIN POSITIVE FEATURES

The most important positive feature of the Agreement is that a serious beginning has been made to bring agriculture into the normal discipline of the international trading rules. Some major developed countries had been subsidising their agricultural products for a long time with the result that other agricultural exporters were put to great disadvantage. Now there is a commitment to cut down the subsidy both on the production and export.

A unique positive feature of the Agreement is that even such measures as subsidies have been covered by the specific commitment of reduction from year to year. In other areas generally, only the tariffs are given such coverage of reduction commitment.

MAIN DEFICIENCIES AND IMBALANCES

(I) *Unfair obligation*

The general scheme of the commitment in the Agreement is that those countries which have been using measures for import restraint and domestic subsidy, were required to reduce the levels respectively by 36% and 20%. The budgetary outlay and the quantity of export covered by the export subsidy were expected to be reduced respectively by 36% and 21%. The levels for the developing countries were two-thirds of these percentages. It means that those countries which were using these measures would be able to retain quite a big portion of them even up to the end of the implementation period. However, those countries which were not using these measures earlier, are prohibited from using these in future, beyond the *de minimis* limits. This is patently unfair in the sense that countries distorting the market in the past are allowed to distort it up to a substantial extent, whereas those that have refrained from doing so in the past are totally prohibited to use these measures in the future.

(II)   Need for domestic food production

The Agreement is based on the rationale of open international trade in the agriculture sector. It thus presupposes the supremacy of the price system and the comparative advantage operating in this sector. The implication is that a country must import its agricultural products from those countries that produce them more cheaply than its own production. In theory it may be all right; in practice it can be disastrous for the food products of developing countries.

Countries that have enough foreign exchange can depend on the import of cheap food products, but those that are short of foreign exchange will be in serious difficulty if they have always to depend on imports for their essential and staple food items. Most of the developing countries have persistent shortage of foreign exchange. In such a situation, if they depend mainly on food imports, their population may sometimes face starvation, as they may not have enough foreign exchange to buy food abroad. A country can delay the import of industrial products for a while, but it cannot delay providing essential food items to its people.

In this context, it may be wiser for these countries to have as much domestic production of necessary food items as their land resources permit. It is desirable, even if the domestic production is more costly compared to the import of the food articles.

(III)   Non-commercial farming

In a large number of developing countries with agricultural land, agriculture is generally not taken up as a commercial venture, though there may be some small pockets of commercial farming. Many farmers take to cultivation as they got the land in the form of ancestral property and they have no other profession. This is in the nature of subsistence cultivation at the household level. Similarly, there are large numbers of small farmers in most of the developing countries.

It is extremely difficult to harmonise these special characteristics in many developing countries with the operation of price mechanism and the commercial nature of agriculture, which are the basic underlying principles in the Agreement on Agriculture. Livelihood of the households may be threatened on a colossal scale in developing countries, if these farmers are exposed to international competition in agricultural products.

(IV) High tariffs in developed countries

In the process of tariffication, several developed countries have kept the tariffs in their schedules very high. Some examples have been given above. It makes the import prospect really meagre.

(V)   Net food importing countries

The problems of the net food importing developing countries have been recognised, but as mentioned above, no concrete action is mentioned in the Ministerial Decision. The result is that no concrete action on this problem has been taken so far, even though sympathies have been expressed time and again.

(VI)   Correctness of schedules

The modality paper has not been made a part of the Agreement; as such the provisions included therein are not enforceable. One relied on the countries themselves to prepare their schedules based on the relevant facts. However, some studies have indicated that some of these calculations might not have been totally accurate. All this was done in a hurry; and it is likely that the countries did not have enough resources to prepare accurate schedules in such a short time. The time for verification was also short. Hence one cannot be sure that the provisions of the modality paper have been fully implemented.

(VII) Tariff quotas

When ordinary tariffs are high, sometimes countries allow imports up to some quantity at comparatively low tariff levels. These quantities are called tariff quotas. Beyond the tariff quota, the imports are subject to the ordinary rates of tariff.

In the Agreement on Agriculture tariff quotas are to be allocated for three purposes, viz., (i) current access opportunity, i.e., providing the opportunity for annual imports equal to the average annual imports for the years 1986-1988, as well as protecting the import opportunities in bilateral or plurilateral agreements, (ii) general minimum access opportunity, i.e., providing opportunity for imports up to a minimum percentage of domestic consumption in the years 1986-1988 and (iii) minimum access opportunity as a result of special treatment. Only four countries have availed themselves of the special treatment mentioned in point (iii) and that also for only one or two products. Hence one need not deliberate much on it for the current discussion. The access opportunity as described in points (i) and (ii) above has to be provided by low tariffs up to a certain quantity of imports. The tariff quotas to protect the access as a result of bilateral or plurilateral agreements will naturally be country-specific. But for other cases of access opportunities, the tariff quota should be global and not specific to countries, so that all countries have the opportunity of utilising the quotas.

In the tariff quotas in agriculture, however, some developed countries have mixed up various elements of access opportunities and have liberally provided for country-specific tariff quotas. Thus other countries do not have the possibility to utilise these access opportunities.

(VIII) Uncertainty about specific domestic support

As mentioned above, the commitment on domestic support is to limit it within the ceiling mentioned in the schedule. A country can modulate the choice of the product and the rate of subsidy, depending on its own need. This keeps the exporters in other countries in uncertainty; thus they have some handicap in planning their own exports.

(IX) Subsidised food stock of developing countries

The subsidy provided by developing countries in purchase of food for stocking and public distribution is exempt from the reduction commitment; but the difference between the purchase price and the external reference price has to be included in the calculation of the Aggregate Measurement of Support (AMS). The AMS is mentioned in the schedule of the country and it signifies that the support cannot exceed that level in that year. As mentioned earlier, it means that a country, choosing to subsidise the food purchase for stocking will have to reduce subsidies on some other items so as to limit the subsidy to the level of the AMS in that year. This would be possible anyway even without this special dispensation; hence this provision which seemingly appears to be a special favour for developing countries is actually not so.

(X)   Discrimination in due-restraint provision

The Agreement on Agriculture provides for due restraint on action against subsidies. There are two categories of subsidies which are covered by it. One set is covered by Article 6 of the Agreement. This includes items like investment subsidy and input subsidy of developing countries. Another set is covered by Annex 2 of the Agreement which includes items like government services programmes, direct payment to producers, income insurance programmes, crop insurance programmes, structural adjustment assistance etc. The second set is generally prevalent in developed countries. In the provisions for due restraint, these two categories are treated differently.

The second set of subsidies, generally prevalent in developed countries, has been exempt from countervailing duty and countermeasures. The first set which contains some important subsidies of developing countries has not got such an exemption. In fact in this case it is just mentioned that due restraint should be shown in initiating countervailing duty investigations. It is in the nature of suggestion and not an obligation.

REQUIRED IMPROVEMENTS

(i)   In order to bring in some fairness in the system of commitment for reduction of import restraint, domestic support and export subsidy, it may be desirable to remove the prohibition on those countries that have not included these measures in their schedules. So far the exemption is up to the *de minimis* level. But considering that the countries having these measures are able to retain the restraints and subsidisation almost up to 65 to 80%, it is desirable to permit the others also to take new measures up to the levels substantially higher than the *de minimis* levels.

(ii)   For developing countries which do not have comfortable foreign exchange on a stable basis for purchase of imported food for their population, it should be permissible to encourage and develop their domestic food production; and to that extent they should be permitted to protect their production against cheap import and provide domestic support to the production. This proposition is very much different from the BOP provisions, which are meant to tackle the BOP problem and are necessarily of temporary nature.

(iii) Similarly, there should be flexibility regarding import restraint and domestic subsidy for the protection of and support to household subsistence farming and small-scale farming in countries where such farming is very much prevalent.

(iv)   There should be a provision for ceilings on the peaks of tariffs in developed countries. Side by side, there should be tariff quotas with lower tariffs.

(v)   The modalities which guided the commitments should be given some formal recognition, so that the conformity of the commitments with the modalities can be improved. Countries could be requested to check up their schedules in this light once again. This process can be more effective, if there is also a provision for verification of schedules once again by other countries.

(vi)   For the net food importing developing countries, there should be specific and concrete decisions regarding food aid and soft loans to buy food in the international market. Countries which are consistently net exporters of food products should be able to shoulder this burden.

(vii) Tariff quotas should be made global, except in some very exceptional cases. If country quotas follow bilateral agreements, the global tariff quotas should be an additionality over these country quotas, to be shared by those that are not covered by the country quotas.

(viii) There should be some predictability about the specific products and rates in the case of domestic support. One way it could be done is to ask the countries to make their plans of distribution of the domestic support within the ceilings a few years in advance. Perhaps an announcement of the subsidy plans could be made, for example, for three years at a time.

(ix) The subsidy provided by developing countries for the purchase of food products for public stocking should be excluded from the AMS, as in the case of other exempted subsidies.

(x) The subsidies covered by Article 6 of the Agreement, particularly the investment subsidy and input subsidy of developing countries, should have the benefit of exemption from countervailing duty and countermeasure as in the case of the subsidies listed in Annex 2 to the Agreement.

TEXTILES

The sector of textiles has been unique in GATT. And in some respects it continues to remain unique in the WTO system as well. This sector has exposed the double standards of developed countries in their assertion of confidence in the free play of market forces.

The textile sector has remained under a special regime in derogation of the normal GATT rules for nearly a quarter of a century. When exports from some developing countries started gaining ground in the sixties and the domestic textile industries in the major developed countries found themselves outpaced in competition, they pressurised their governments into seeking special dispensations from the developing exporting countries. The latter group of countries were persuaded to agree to an orderly marketing arrangement in which the normal rules of free export and import were temporarily suspended. The developing exporting countries agreed to restrain their export to levels bilaterally agreed on under the framework of a multilateral agreement.

The multilateral agreement was earlier called the Short-Term Arrangement and later it became the Long-Term Arrangement. During those days it covered only products of cotton fibre. Later woollen and synthetic-fibre products were included and the arrangement was popularly called the Multi-Fibre Agreement (MFA). More formally, it was called the Arrangement for the International Trade in Textiles and Clothing.

Developed countries had asked for this special dispensation on a temporary basis, so that their industry could have time to adjust to the new situation of declining competitiveness. The expectation of the developing countries was that these industries in the developed countries would finally close down, and investment and resources would shift to other more viable sectors. MFA, however, continued being extended every four years; and industries in this sector in developed countries started improving their competitiveness with the protective shield of the MFA. Even then developed countries did not agree to revert to the normal rules of GATT.

Finally, in the Uruguay Round the developed countries agreed to negotiate on ending the MFA regime, but they wanted some price for it in terms of liberalisation in this sector in developing countries. It was a strange case of aggressive negotiation in the international trade. The developed countries should have normally compensated the developing exporting countries for the loss caused to them by the special restrictive regime in this sector for nearly three decades. But, quite to the contrary, they insisted on developing countries giving them compensation for removing the MFA. Finally a compromise was reached and the Uruguay Round resulted in the Agreement on Textiles and Clothing.

MAIN ELEMENTS OF THE AGREEMENT

The most important provision in the Agreement is that the MFA would end on 31 December 1994, and the special arrangement on textiles would finally be terminated on 1 January 2005, when this sector will be fully integrated in the normal rules of WTO Agreements.

The restraints on imports imposed under the MFA before the end of 1994 will be continuing, but these will be progressively liberalised. Liberalisation will be carried out by the countries imposing MFA restrictions in four stages. The final stage will be on 1 January 2005, when all remaining restrictions will be terminated. At the earlier three stages, which fall respectively on 1 January of 1995, 1998 and 2002, the importing countries will liberalise some products accounting for certain specified percentages of the import of the totality of textile products mentioned in the annex to the Agreement. These liberalised products will revert to the normal rules of WTO Agreements. Besides, there will be a modest rise in the permissible import levels of the restricted products from year to year till these are fully liberalised.

An importing country may use transitional safeguard provision to impose new restraints. However, the products which have been covered by the liberalisation process cannot be the object of transitional safeguard provision; only the normal safeguard provision of the WTO Agreements will apply to those products.

There are stringent provisions regarding circumvention of restraints. Circumvention, for example, could take place by an exporter falsely declaring the country of origin or the description of a product. On the suspicion of circumvention relating to the origin of a product, the importing country will hold an investigation and on being satisfied about the circumvention, it can impose unilateral measures on such imports, which may include denial of entry of the product, adjusting the quantity of import against the quota level of the country determined to be the true origin, etc.

The Textile Monitoring Body (TMB) has been established to oversee the implementation of the Agreement and also to examine the disputes between parties. If a country continues to be dissatisfied with the decisions of the TMB even on a second representation, it may take the matter to the Dispute Settlement Body of WTO which will start the panel process.

A significant provision of the Agreement relates to the expectation of the balance of rights and obligations in the textile sector. If a country feels that the balance is not ensured in respect of another country, it may refer the matter to the Council for Trade in Goods, which has the responsibility of ensuring the balance.

IMPORTANT POSITIVE FEATURES

The most important positive feature is that there has been an agreement to wind up the special trade regime in the textile sector. From the way the textile lobby was operating in major developed countries, it was apprehended that this sector would always continue to be under a special umbrella of rules. In fact attempts had been made several times to introduce similar special regimes in some other sectors as well. But now the Agreement makes it clear that the MFA is over and the continuing restrictions will be decidedly terminated on a specified date.

The transitional safeguard provisions are an improvement over the similar provisions in the MFA. Some important points to be noted in this connection are the following:

(i)   In the MFA, price of the product was included in the factors to be considered in market disruption. Now the "low price" criterion is not there in the pre-conditions for the transitional safeguard. This is beneficial for the developing countries, as they had been the targets on the ground of the comparatively low prices of their products.

(ii)   In identifying the source (country) of import causing serious damage, the comparison of imports from various sources will have to be made and market share of different sources (countries) of supply will have to be taken into account. This process will protect developing countries from being singled out as sources of serious damage.

The role of the TMB has been strengthened. The Members of WTO must endeavour to accept the recommendations of this body.

PROBLEMS WITH THE AGREEMENT

(I)   *Progressive liberalisation process*

The experience of the first stage of liberalisation effective on 1 January 1995 has been disappointing. Major importing developed countries have technically fulfilled their obligation of liberalising 16% of their import of items covered by the Annex; but in fact they have not done any real liberalisation, as the products liberalised by them were never under any restraint in those countries.

The problem lies with the content of the Annex, which contains a large number of items which are not under restraint under the MFA, and some of them never have been. The importing countries have chosen to include in the first stage of liberalisation only those products from this list which were never under restraint. Thus the commitment of the prescribed percentage of products in the Annex being brought under general GATT 1994 discipline has been fulfilled; but the exporting countries have derived no benefit, as these items were quite free anyway.

The developed importing countries have not reacted helpfully and sympathetically to the criticism of their action in this first stage. The natural apprehension is that they will continue with the technical fulfilment of their obligation without actually doing any real liberalisation, if they can help it. And the Annex contains "free" items in such substantial measure that several major importing countries can continue with this tactic even in the second stage of liberalisation on 1 January 1998.

(II)   *The operation of the transitional safeguard*

The existing provisions of the transitional safeguard, even though much improved compared to the provisions of the MFA, have not been able to prevent some major importing developed countries from initiating a spate of cases of safeguard action. The specific caution mentioned in the Agreement that transitional safeguard will be only sparingly used, does not seem to have weight with these major importing developed countries. The criteria for the transitional safe-guard action have been ignored in these cases.

(III) Sectoral balance of rights and obligations

The stipulation of sectoral balance of rights and obligations as explicitly mentioned in this Agreement is a totally new feature in the WTO system nor did it exist in its predecessor, the GATT system. This whole system depends on the underlying principle of overall balance of rights and obligations. And it was this feature which prompted the WTO Agreements being declared a single undertaking. The basic idea is that in this comprehensive system, some countries derive benefits in some sectors, while others derive benefits in other sectors. It will undermine the system very much if separate balances are sought in isolated areas. This is precisely what has been done in the textile sector and it may sow the seed of long-term damage to the system.

(IV) Problems of end-loading of liberalisation

Though the determined and declared aim is to integrate this sector into the normal WTO Agreements, the process of liberalisation as envisaged in the Agreement does not appear to be helpful enough in having this aim achieved. As much as half of the products are left till the very end to be covered by liberalisation. And taking into account the dismal performance of the major importing countries in implementation of this provision in actual terms, the task appears much more difficult. A situation will emerge when the textile industry in the developed countries will suddenly be faced with a major challenge at the end of the transition period. And then there may be reluctance and difficulties, and consequent pressures once again on the governments of developed countries to perpetuate the special rules in this sector.

There is no provision for concrete positive action by developed importing countries regarding structural adjustment in this sector. There is a grave need for planned action for structural adjustment in this sector in these countries, and as such, specific provisions should have been made in the Agreement in this regard. This would have facilitated the process of progressive liberalisation, particularly towards the end of the liberalisation period.

NECESSARY IMPROVEMENTS

(i)   The process of liberalisation should be expedited in real terms and not only in the technical sense. A decision should be taken that the importing countries will accelerate the process in the second stage of liberalisation, so that the inclusion of only free items in the first stage gets duly compensated. The second stage of liberalisation should compensate for the deficiencies of the first stage mentioned above.

(ii)   In the operation of the transitional safeguard the guideline in the Agreement that it should be sparingly used has apparently not worked. Some more effective means are needed to have this guideline followed. One way could be to lay down a maximum number of possible initiation of actions by an importing country against a specific exporting country during the course of the transition period. Another more radical way may be to provide for some compensation, in cases where the initiation of action by an importing country against an exporting country has been repeatedly found by the TMB to be wrong.

(iii)   It is desirable to remove the concept of the sectoral balance of rights and obligations from this Agreement. This step will be in the interest of the integrity of the WTO system; otherwise, the apprehension is that there may be demands in future for such sectoral balance in other sectors or limited isolated balances in specific subjects. A near-universal body like the WTO with so much diversity of interests cannot subsist on such islands of balances.

(iv)   There should be a provision for major importing countries monitoring the structural adjustment in this sector in their economies. And this move should be under the scrutiny of the TMB. It is necessary to encourage and even enforce structural adjustment in this sector. Otherwise at the end of the transition period, the WTO Members may suddenly find that the textile industries in developed countries are not able to absorb the consequences of the total abolition of import restraints in their countries.

CHAPTER 7

NON-TRADITIONAL ISSUES

THE disciplines of GATT have been traditionally limited to the goods sector as the trade in goods was an important part of international transactions. However, towards the early eighties, some other sectors started playing a very important role, and vast potential was opening up in these areas. Three sectors were particularly important, viz., services, high technology and investment. The first two were, in fact, going through a phase of a major revolution in which the pace of advance was phenomenal. These were also having a profound impact on the goods sector, as production processes were undergoing rapid changes as a result of their interaction with services and high technology.

Major developed countries perceived very high potential of growth in their services sector, if they were able to export services to other countries, including developing countries, some of which were on a high-growth path. It was therefore considered necessary to ensure free flow of services across the border. There was no risk in this process to the services sector in the developed countries which had already developed to levels where they would not have any competition from the services firms of developing countries. Hence liberalisation in the services sector was of great advantage to them without any risks involved.

Similarly, the technology was developing at breakneck speed in the developed countries, and it was necessary to protect this development by curtailing parallel development elsewhere. This needed a regime of high protection of intellectual property rights (IPRs) all over the world. Here, too, the risk was not high, as the protection to the intellectual property of the IPR-holders of developing countries would give no challenge, since there are so few of them.

In this context, major developed countries started very intense moves for liberalisation in the services sector and ensuring free flow of services across the border as well as for the protection in the field of intellectual property, i.e., high technology. The inherent conceptual contradiction in these two moves did not bother them at all. On the one hand, they were seeking liberalisation in the services sector, while, on the other hand, they were asking for protection in the sector of high technology.

It was also perceived in major developed countries that their investors would be able to get much higher returns if they had the opportunity to invest in developing countries. The scope of enhancing the return in their own countries had very much diminished.

These were the main reasons for the powerful multinational firms in developed countries to urge their governments to push for negotiations and agreements in these areas. GATT was considered an appropriate forum where developed countries had considerable clout. Besides, it would also ensure an effective enforcement of the obligations through the dispute settlement mechanism of GATT. Retaliatory action in the sector of goods would hurt the developing countries, whereas such action in the areas of services or intellectual property rights would not.

The first moves were made in the GATT Ministerial Meeting of November 1982. These three subjects were very aggressively pushed by major developed countries. In the fields of investment and high technology, there were differences among the major developed countries, but in the area of services they were very much united. Hence the pressure on developing countries to start negotiations in GATT for liberalisation of services was much stronger than in other areas. In fact, the other areas were given up by the proponents towards the end. The strong moves in the services sector, however, continued right till the end. At that time developing countries were much more united and had some common perception of their interests. They stoutly opposed these moves. Consequently, the developed countries did not succeed in introducing services in GATT. There was an agreement, however, that countries would conduct their own national studies of services and exchange information on this subject, and later it would be seen if a multilateral discipline in this field would be appropriate.

Finally, when the idea of a new round of negotiations in GATT was floated, these three subjects were revived. And when Uruguay Round was launched, these areas were taken up for negotiations. In the final result, the agreement on investment was subsumed in the normal GATT, covering only the existing discipline of the trade in goods. But detailed agreements were concluded involving disciplines in the areas of services and intellectual property rights.

SERVICES

MAIN ELEMENTS OF THE AGREEMENT

The General Agreement on Trade in Services (GATS) lays down certain basic disciplines and provides a framework for negotiations on the liberalisation of services sectors. Before the Agreement was formally put into effect along with the other WTO Agreements, negotiations took place among countries for commitments on market access and national treatment (non-discrimination as between foreign service supplier and domestic service supplier). These commitments were included in the country schedules and formed an integral part of the Agreement.

The Agreement has broadly two types of discipline: first, that relating to all services sectors, and second, sectoral commitments, i.e., disciplines relating to specific sectors. The former sets of disciplines are included in the text of the main Agreement, and are called general commitments. The latter, i.e., the specific commitments or sectoral commitments emerge out of negotiations among countries based on a frame given in the text of the Agreement, and, as indicated above, these are included in the country schedules of specific commitments.

In specific commitments, countries lay down the terms, limitations and conditions under which services will be allowed access to their markets. They may also prescribe conditions and qualifications on the national treatment of foreign services. In different sectors of services, different terms and conditions can be laid down. The final set of terms, limitations, conditions and qualifications of a country will depend on the agreement of other countries. Only when the proposals of a country in this regard are accepted by other partners, can these be inscribed by it in its schedule. Procedures have been laid down for the modification of the schedules in future. A framework has also been included for future negotiations among countries on specific commitments.

Among the general commitments, the most important one is on most-favoured-nation (mfn) treatment, i.e., non-discrimination as between services and service-suppliers of various Members of the WTO. Services will enjoy mfn treatment, except if a country has stipulated some exceptions right at the beginning, and recorded these exceptions in a schedule meant for this purpose. After the schedules have been finalised and made part of the Agreement, a Member is not free to have any other exceptions in respect of the mfn commitment. If it wants to have any other exception, it will have to follow the process of getting a waiver for this purpose, which is very cumbersome and difficult.

The provisions for the disciplines on safeguard and subsidy in this sector will be negotiated later. There is, however, a provision for restrictions in case of BOP problems, which is similar to the provision applicable to goods.

In the negotiations for the liberalisation in various services sectors, there are special provisions relating to developing countries. They will be required to liberalise fewer sectors and fewer types of transactions. They will have the flexibility to expand market access in line with their development situation. They can attach conditions to market access aimed at strengthening the capacity, efficiency and competitiveness of their domestic services as well as improvement of their access to distribution channels and information networks. Besides, special attention is to be given to the liberalisation of market access in sectors and modes of supply of export interest to developing countries.

PROBLEMS AND IMBALANCES

(I)   *Asymmetry between capital and labour*

There are specific provisions for free movement of capital associated with the commitments in the Agreement on Services, whereas there is no such provision regarding the movement of labour. If a Member has undertaken a market access commitment for permitting the supply of service from another country and if the cross-border movement of capital is an essential part of the service itself, the Member is thereby committed to allow such movement of capital. Further, if a Member undertakes a market access commitment for permitting the supply of services through commercial presence, it is thereby committed to allow related transfers of capital into its territory. Besides, it is also laid down in the Agreement that a Member must not apply restrictions on international transfers and payments for current transactions relating to its specific commitments. All this may appear reasonable; but lack of similar provisions for the movement of labour clearly brings about asymmetry and imbalance.

(II)   *Provisions for developing countries*

The provisions to take care of the concerns of developing countries are being totally ignored. In spite of these provisions which have been mentioned above, major developed countries have been expecting high commitments from developing countries for liberalisation. Thus these provisions are not being respected. This tendency has been recently noticed in some sectoral negotiations. For example, during the negotiation on financial services, major developed countries insisted on high levels of concessions from some developing countries.

There is no mechanism in the Agreement for ensuring compliance with these provisions which are really mandatory.

(III) Asymmetry of sectors for priority negotiations

The sectors which have been undertaken for negotiations for liberalisations after the coming into force of WTO Agreements are generally those which are of interest to developed countries, e.g., financial services, insurance, maritime transport etc. Sectors in which developing countries have export interest have not been taken up. This has been so, in spite of the fact that Members are required under the Agreement to take specific commitments to liberalise market access in sectors of export interest to developing countries, as mentioned above.

(IV) Impracticability of sectoral negotiations

After the WTO Agreements came into force, there were negotiations in specific services sectors one by one. These negotiations have not been successful. In fact, there is a basic flaw in holding sectoral negotiations, as the interests of the participants are likely to clash in individual sectors. The negotiations would have been more result-oriented, if a number of sectors of different types had been taken together for negotiations. In that case, there would have been a good possibility of complementarity of interests across the sectors. A country would have been prepared to offer concessions in some sectors in exchange for the concessions of others in other sectors.

NECESSARY IMPROVEMENTS

(i)   Movement of labour should at least be given the same special consideration as has been given to the movement of capital. The argument that the movement of labour is related to immigration cannot be used to give less favourable treatment to labour. If the movement of capital associated with specific commitments is to be mandatorily allowed, there is no reason why the movement of labour associated similarly with some specific commitments should not be made a mandatory commitment.

(ii)   The Committee on Services should have a mechanism for monitoring the observance of the special provisions relating to developing countries. It should be the responsibility of this Committee to ensure that these provisions are fully followed. The intervention of the Committee is particularly important and necessary as it may be impractical to enforce these provisions through the dispute settlement process.

(iii)   The Committee on Services should ensure that sectors of interest to developing countries are also taken up for negotiation along with the sectors which are currently being taken up.

(iv)   In fact, the movement in the sectoral negotiations will gain pace if a large number of sectors across the board are taken up for simultaneous negotiations so that there can be a possibility of some give-and-take among these sectors.

TRADE-RELATED INTELLECTUAL PROPERTY RIGHTS (TRIPS)

MAIN ELEMENTS OF THE AGREEMENT ON TRIPS

This Agreement essentially protects intellectual property rights and lays down minimum standards of protection which all countries must have. A country is free to have higher levels of protection. The areas of intellectual property covered by the Agreement are patents, copyright and related rights, trademarks, geographical indications, industrial designs, layout-designs of integrated circuits and undisclosed information.

There are some provisions in the Agreement which are applicable to all areas of IPR covered by the Agreement. The important ones among these are the following:

(i)   The broad objectives of the Agreement are promotion of technological innovation, transfer and dissemination of technology, contribution to the mutual advantage of producers and users of technological knowledge conducive to social and economic welfare and contribution to the balance of rights and obligations.

(ii)   The most-favoured-nation treatment, i.e., non-discrimination as between the nationals of different Members, and the national treatment, i.e., non-discrimination as between the nationals of any other Member country and domestic nationals, have to be adopted by all Members.

(iii)   Members may take corrective measures against licensing practices and conditions which restrain competition, as these may have adverse effect on trade and may impede transfer and dissemination of technology.

(iv)   Effective administrative and judicial arrangements have to be made to enforce the IPRs.

(v)   The implementation of the Agreement in various countries must be ensured through appropriate domestic legislation.

There are specific provisions relating to each of the seven types of IPRs covered by the Agreement. These are described in brief below.

PATENTS

Inventions will be eligible for patenting, if these are new, involve an inventive step and are capable of industrial production. Both products and processes are eligible for patenting. Besides, the patent rights will be enjoyed without discrimination regarding the place of invention, the field of technology and whether products are imported or domestically produced. Diagnostic, therapeutic and surgical methods, plants and animals and essentially biological processes for the production of plants and animals need not be patented. Besides, patent can be denied on the ground of public order, morality, protection of human, animal and plant life or health, and protection of environment.

Micro-organisms, like bacteria, viruses, fungi, algae, protozoa etc. and non-biological and microbiological processes for the production of plants and animals will be eligible for patent.

Even though plants are excluded, the plant varieties have to be protected either by patenting or by some effective *sui generis* system.

The minimum term of the patent is for twenty years from the date of filing.

The patent on a product confers the right on the patent-holder to prevent any other person to make, use, sell or import the product without the consent of the patent-holder. The process patent confers the right to prevent a person, who does not have the consent of the patent-holder, from using the process and also from using, selling or importing the product produced by that process.

The obligation on the patent-holder is that he or she must disclose all information clearly and completely so that an expert can carry out the same invention.

There can be limited exception to the patent right, e.g., for the use of the patented product or process for experimental purposes in pursuit of further scientific development.

There can be non-voluntary licensing, which is also called compulsory licensing, i.e., the licence to use the patent without the consent of the patent-holder under certain circumstances, but some conditions will have to be followed, particularly in respect of the compensation to the patent-holder.

COPYRIGHT AND RELATED RIGHTS

Copyright is granted to authors in their literary or artistic work or similar work. The related rights, also called neighbouring rights, cover generally the rights of performing artists in their performances, the rights of producers of phonograms (i.e., sound recordings) in their phonograms and the rights of broadcasting organisations in their radio and television programmes. Computer programmes are covered by the discipline of copyright.

There are various minimum terms for these rights. For example, the term of copyright is the life of the author and fifty years after his or her death. In the case of cinematographic works, the term is fifty years after the work has been made available to the public with the consent of the author. The term of photographic work is twenty-five years from the making of the work. The term of the protection to performers and producers of phonograms is fifty years from the end of the year of fixation or performance. The term for the broadcasting organisation is twenty years from the end of the year of the broadcast.

It is permissible to provide for limitations or exceptions to the copyright in special cases.

TRADEMARK

A trademark is defined as any sign which distinguishes the goods or services of one undertaking from those of the others. The initial minimum term is for seven years. There is a provision for renewal for the same term and there is no limitation on the number of times the renewal can take place.

GEOGRAPHICAL INDICATIONS

Geographical indication identifies a product as originating in a particular place to which its quality, reputation or other characteristics are essentially attributable. It is particularly prevalent in the case of wine and spirits. Members have to provide for the prevention of the use of means indicating that a product originates in a place other than the true place of origin, and thereby misleading the public as to the true origin of the product.

INDUSTRIAL DESIGNS

Industrial design refers to the features concerning the look of an article, for example, the shape, ornamentation, pattern, configuration etc. Members are required to provide for the protection of industrial designs, if these are new and original.

Considering the importance of industrial designs in the textile sector for developing countries, there is a provision that requirements, particularly in respect of costs, examination or publication, should not unreasonably impair the opportunity to get protection.

The owners of the industrial designs should have the right to prevent the use of the design without their consent. Limited exceptions to the rights are permissible.

LAYOUT-DESIGNS OF INTEGRATED CIRCUITS

To qualify for protection, the layout-designs have to be original. Reproduction of the layout-design, selling or importing the layout-design, and also selling or importing an article containing the layout - design, without the authorisation of the right-holder will be illegal. There are some exceptions, e.g., reproduction for private purposes or for research etc.

UNDISCLOSED INFORMATION

It relates to secret information with a person or a firm, e.g., a trade secret, or information lodged with government in the case of pharma-ceutical or agricultural products. The persons having the undisclosed information should have the right to prevent the disclosure or acqui-sition or use of the information without the consent of the person possessing it. However, for this purpose, the information must be secret, it must have a commercial value and the person having the possession has taken reasonable steps to keep it a secret.

PROBLEMS

The most problematic of the IPRs has been the patent; hence the problems and possible improvements are being discussed with par-ticular reference to patents, though some other areas also will get covered. These are all new areas introduced in the sphere of trade policy and there is yet no experience in these fields. It is likely that problems may arise in the course of the implementation of the Agreement; at that time the Committee will no doubt consider the problems and try to find solutions. Some obvious problems as perceptible now are discussed below.

(I)   *Objectives not incorporated in specific provisions*

The objectives of the Agreement mentioned above have not been incorporated into specific provisions of the Agreement. For example, the transfer and dissemination of technology and contribution to the mutual advantage of producers and users of technological knowledge conducive to social and economic welfare have not been translated into actual specific provisions in the Agreement.

(II)   *Unbalanced protection*

The conflict of interests in the IPR field is between the interest of the innovators and that of the consumers. Another set of conflicts may arise between the interest of well-established IPR-holders and new and small innovators. An IPR protection regime should generally try to balance these interests. In this context, the Agreement is grossly deficient. It merely provides for the protection of the interests of the IPR-holders, without any significant balancing factors to protect the interests of the consumers of intellectual property. Similarly there is nothing in the Agreement which will take care of the interests of new and small innovators who try to make innovations on the margin. The entire focus of the Agreement is to seek maximum possible gain for the established patent-holders.

The provision of the product patent will dampen the initiatives of new and small innovators who might have tried to find alternative methods of production of the same product, if only the process, and not the product, had been patented. It will also discourage investment in research, particularly in developing countries, where financial and physical resources for research are limited. Investors will rightly fear that they have to undertake very high risks. The targeted product may be invented earlier by a competitor, and then the whole investment will be lost, as any alternative process of production of the product will not be allowed. In the absence of the provision for the product patent, this investor in the developing country would still have the hope that his/her investment might result in the invention of an alternative process for producing the product.

(III) Problems in harmonisation of minimum protection

The balance between these interests should be decided according to the socio-economic background of the individual country. It will depend a good deal on the perception of public interest by each country in the context of its socio-economic objectives. As such, providing a minimum standard of protection to be followed by all countries appears unreasonable. Some countries may consider the interests of innovators more important than those of consumers; and they will be quite happy with a high standard of protection of IPR. But some other countries may consider the interests of the consumers more predominant; and thus they would like to have a lower standard of protection and also they would like to curb the malpractices of the monopoly which the IPR system necessarily generates.

(IV) Risks to consumers regarding layout-designs of integrated circuits

In the part of the Agreement relating to the protection of the Layout-designs of Integrated Circuits, there is an onerous responsibility on the innocent users of a product which is illegally incorporating an integrated circuit. After the illegal incorporation is brought to his/her notice, he/she has to pay to the right-holder a reasonable royalty. The implication will be clear by an example. Let us suppose that a consumer purchases a washing machine in the market and starts using it. After some time, if it is brought to the notice of the consumer that the producer of the machine had incorporated an integrated circuit illegally, this consumer will then have to pay royalty to the person that holds right for the integrated circuit. This is an extremely risky and inconvenient provision for consumers in general who never bother to find out which type of integrated circuits or other parts have been used in the machine. It was for this reason that the Washington Treaty (IPIC Treaty) had been opposed and was not concluded. Now this provision has been included in the Agreement on TRIPs.

(V)   Bias in favour of raising protection level

A bias has been introduced in favour of raising the levels of protection. This is to be found not in the Agreement on TRIPs, but in the provision for amendments in Article X of the Agreement Establishing the WTO (WTO Agreement). It provides for simple adoption of amendments in a Ministerial Conference without formal acceptance process, if the amendments relate to raising the levels of protection. There is no such corresponding provision relating to lowering of the protection levels.

NECESSARY IMPROVEMENTS

(i)   It is necessary to incorporate specific provisions in the implementable parts of the Agreement which will fulfil the objectives of the Agreement. For example, in respect of granting the patents, it may be laid down that the Members may refuse patent or impose conditions on patents if such action is considered necessary for the fulfilment of the objectives of the Agreement.

(ii)   There should be some specific provisions in the Agreement taking care of the consumers explicitly. For example, a provision for the possibility of price control, in case of unduly high price of the patented product, will be quite reasonable.

(iii)   Though in practice it is too late, it is still necessary to suggest that insistence on common adoption of the minimum level of protection of IPR, ignoring the varying perceptions of public interest in different countries, is unfair. There should be the scope for a country to differ from the common minimum standards for defensible valid reasons.

(iv)   At various places in the Agreement, there is scope for exercise of discretion. It will be utilised by various countries to reflect their own perceptions of public interests in their respective legislations. There may be an initial enthusiasm among the advocates of high IPR protection to challenge these moves and rush to the Dispute Settlement Body. Such enthusiasm will not be correct. It will be appropriate to exercise due restraint and be liberal in allowing the countries to exercise their discretion in the way they consider best.

(v) The bias in favour of raising the levels of protection should be removed from the procedure for amendments.

CHAPTER 8

SOME OTHER PROVISIONS

THERE are several other areas where deficiencies and imbalances exist and improvements are needed. Only the important ones have been covered in the previous chapters.

In this chapter, two other areas needing special attention will be discussed, viz., (i) neo-protectionism through exceptions, standards and sanitary and phytosanitary (sps) measures and (ii) Part IV of GATT 1994.

NEO-PROTECTIONISM

EXCEPTIONS, STANDARDS AND SPS

There was a time in the past, when protection to the domestic industry was provided by developed countries through the grey area measures. As it came up for persistent criticism in GATT and outside, the technique was changed and these countries started providing large-scale protection through anti-dumping action. Now anti-dumping measures have also come up for considerable criticism, and rules have also been made more objective. Hence the new tools of protectionism are being used. These are the general exceptions (Article XX of GATT 1994), standards and sanitary and phytosanitary measures.

There have been well-known recent cases of restraint on tuna import, because the devices for catching tuna also catch and endanger dolphins. Also there have been restraints on the import of shrimp, because the turtles also get caught in the nets used for catching shrimp.

Earlier, there have been several cases of import restraints on the ground of the products containing some chemicals considered to be harmful.

CURRENT PROVISIONS FOR RESTRICTIONS

General exceptions contained in Article XX of GATT 1994 permit measures which are necessary to protect human, animal or plant life or health. Here the qualifying term "necessary" is significant. Countries are also permitted to take measures relating to the conservation of exhaustible natural resources if such measures are made effective in conjunction with restrictions on domestic production and consumption.

In respect of the standards, under the Agreement on Technical Barriers to Trade, countries are permitted to have technical regulations to meet legitimate objectives, including the protection of (i) human health or safety, (ii) protection of animal and plant life or health and (iii) protection of environment. One of the main restrictions on such action is that it should not create "unnecessary obstacles to international trade".

Besides, the Agreement on the Application of Sanitary and Phytosanitary Measures permits actions to protect human, animal and plant life or health from harmful chemicals, organisms, pests etc. Here the limitation is that such measures should be applied only to the extent necessary to protect life or health, and the measures should not be more trade-restrictive than required to achieve an appropriate level of protection.

CURRENT TRENDS OF ENTHUSIASTIC USE

Major developed countries have enthusiastically used these provisions in the recent past to impose restraints on imports, particularly from developing countries. There have been import restraint measures or threat of such measures against the tuna from Canada and Mexico, shrimp from India, some textiles from India, gasoline from Venezuela etc. Earlier, restraints were placed on the products which directly contained some harmful contents. Recently attempts have been made to extend the coverage of restrictions even to such products which are themselves not harmful, but which, in the process of production, are perceived to endanger the environment, e.g., tuna-dolphin, and shrimp-turtle cases. Now there are pressures to enhance the scope further. For example, the import of a processed food product may be sought to be restrained, if during the processing, the environment around the processing plant gets polluted, even if the product itself contains nothing which will harm the human, animal or plant life in the importing country directly.

The problem goes back to the technical barriers, where products and "related" production methods may be covered by the technical regulations. Thus these regulations can impose import restraint on the products and "related" production methods. The term "related" has been understood to mean a situation in which the production method has an effect on the composition of the product. For example, in the case of food products, the production method may be such that harmful chemical residue is left in the product. If during the processing, the environment gets polluted, for example, by the smoke or the effluent discharge from the factory, that adverse situation is not covered by the possible control through technical regulations in the importing country.

The pressures now are such that even factors not traditionally covered by the term "related" should be taken into account.

Another dangerous trend is to change the connotation of "national treatment" in respect of the import of the product which is alleged to be harmful. One important principle so far has been that similar treatment should be given to the imported product and like domestic product. The likeness is decided by the content of the product, its use, its chemical or vegetable origin etc. Hence a particular food product, say strawberry jam, imported to a country would be considered to be a product like the strawberry jam produced in the importing country. If this imported jam has similar content as the domestic jam, there cannot be any discrimination against the imported jam *vis-à-vis* the domestic jam. Of course, if the imported jam contains some harmful chemical which is not present in the domestic jam, the two products would not be considered "like", and, in that case, discrimination between the imported jam and the domestic jam can be permitted.

Now there are pressures to limit the meaning of the "like" product further. Pressures are exerted to disallow national treatment to an imported product, if the production method has resulted in pollution of the environment, even if, on the basis of physical characteristics and use, the imported product and the domestic product are alike. If this move succeeds, the result will be that discriminatory restraints can be imposed on the imported products without imposing similar restrictions on the domestic product, which currently is considered "like" product.

NECESSARY CAUTION

It is important to guard against the unfair use of the general exceptions or the provisions relating to health or environment. There should be no dilution of the present limitations on such measures. Besides, the present multilateral scrutiny in the framework of WTO Agreements must continue. A country should not be given more freedom to take trade restrictive measures on these grounds. The fear is that these measures will turn into real neo-protectionist measures, because of strong lobbies for import restraint.

PART IV OF GATT 1994

Part IV of GATT 1994 is nearly forgotten now. And yet its provisions are as much valid and enforceable as these were earlier. This part of GATT 1994 was introduced in GATT to take care of the special development problems and economic handicaps of developing countries. These provisions were not in the nature of contractual agreement, in the sense that retaliatory action could not be taken if a country did not abide by these provisions. But even then, these provisions have enough force to be enforceable through the various institutions of WTO, if there is a political will among the developed countries to respect these provisions and also the determination among the developing countries to have these special provisions implemented.

MAIN ELEMENTS

These provisions are contained in Articles XXXVI, XXXVII and XXXVIII of GATT 1994. Article XXXVI lays down the broad principles and objectives for special treatment of developing countries. Article XXXVII prescribes the specific actions to be taken towards these objectives and Article XXXVIII stipulates joint action by all Members in support of developing countries.

The essential elements are in Article XXXVII, which has the title "commitments". The commitments start with the following undertaking:

> "The developed contracting parties shall to the fullest extent possible – that is, except when compelling reasons, which may include legal reasons, make it impossible – give effect to the following provisions.........."

It can hardly be doubted that this commitment is quite firm; and a developed country has to be accountable for the implementation of these provisions. If it cannot implement these provisions, it has the onus to clarify what "compelling reasons" made it impossible. Even though this provision may not be contractually enforceable, it is strong enough to call for strict scrutiny of individual cases of departure from the commitments.

Then this Article goes on to prescribe the disciplines and actions, which are the following:

(a)   "accord high priority to the reduction and elimination of barriers to products currently or potentially of particular export interest to less-developed contracting parties (a term used in GATT for developing countries), including customs duties and other restrictions which differentiate unreasonably between such products in their primary and in their processed forms;"

(b)   "refrain from introducing, or increasing the incidence of cus-
        toms duties or non-tariff import barriers on products currently
        or potentially of particular export interest to less-developed
        contracting parties;" and

(c)   "(i) refrain from imposing new fiscal measures, and

        (ii) in any adjustments of fiscal policy accord high priority to the
        reduction and elimination of fiscal measures, which would
        hamper, or which hamper, significantly the growth of consump-
        tion of primary products, in raw or processed form, wholly or
        mainly produced in the territories of less-developed contracting
        parties, and which are applied specifically to those products."

The commitments in this Article further require that the developed contracting parties "shall give active consideration to the adoption of other measures designed to provide greater scope for the
development of imports from the less-developed contracting parties
and collaborate in appropriate international action to this end". The
interpretative note further adds that the "other measures" might
include "steps to promote domestic structural changes, to encourage
the consumption of particular products, or to introduce measures of
trade promotion".

In the context of these clear commitments, which have not lost
their validity or relevance in the slightest, the performance of the
developed countries has been dismal. Instead of making the products
of export interest to developing countries an important focus for
reduction or elimination of tariff and non-tariff barriers, these countries have, in fact, retained comparatively higher tariffs on such products, while reducing and eliminating tariffs on products of special
interest to developed countries. Further, the differentiation in these
barriers still continues between the primary products and those in
processed form. Besides, efforts in the direction of structural change as
mentioned above have never been made. Any suggestion that such
positive steps are necessary meets with a persistent response that
structural change is not the concern of government, it is taken care of
by the market forces. But governments have a clear commitment for
taking action for structural changes.

NEED FOR IMPLEMENTATION OF COMMITMENTS

Considering that most of the developing countries are in no better state now, compared to their predicament at the time these commitments were made by developed countries, it is essential that implementation of these commitments is followed up with determination in all relevant institutions of WTO. Developed countries, individually and collectively, should be formally called upon to follow these provisions scrupulously. A programme of action for each developed country should be worked out, and the implementation of the programme should be monitored in an appropriate forum in the WTO.

All this can be possible only if developing countries, individually and in a group, pursue this issue with persistence and determination. They have to insist on the implementation of these commitments.

CHAPTER 9

ARE IMPROVEMENTS POSSIBLE?

SUGGESTIONS for improvements and words of caution have been given in the previous chapters. The obvious question is whether all this is possible. There is a tendency to ignore the suggestions of interest to developing countries on grounds which vary from time to time. Sometimes these may be described as theoretical and impractical. At others, they may be pronounced as untimely and premature. Whatever the reason, there is usually the tendency not to take the demands of developing countries seriously.

In respect of several of these suggestions, the usual criticism may be that these were the initial maximum position of developing countries, and now that the negotiations are over, they should not be revived. Of course, one is likely to forget conveniently that many of the new proposals of major developed countries were also made during the negotiations and they did not succeed. The developed countries have not hesitated in putting up these proposals again shortly after the negotiations ended. For example, the new proposals on investment were substantially covered by the initial stand of major developed countries, and were not accepted in the negotiations.

One has to appreciate that it is not only in the interest of developing countries that some of the improvements suggested in earlier chapters should be carried out. As indicated in various chapters, these suggestions have been made mainly to remove perceived deficiencies and imbalances. An effort in this direction will strengthen the system.

Questions also naturally arise whether the environment is conducive for engaging in working for these improvements and what strategies will be appropriate. The environment is certainly not very positive.

There has been a significant change in the perception of the statespersons of developed countries. In the sixties and early seventies, they were moved by two main perceptions: first, the real relevance and the imperatives of sincere mutual cooperation between developed and developing countries in the interest of mankind, and second, the post-colonial era's concern for participating in the improvement of the conditions of the peoples that had long suffered. There was a mix of practical wisdom and idealism driving these statespersons.

Now the situation has changed. Some important new features are the following:

(i)   Almost all the developed countries have become more inward-looking. Internal pressures on them have increased, and they are often unable to resist these pressures. More often they tend to cater to short-term needs, thereby ignoring the long-term interests.

(ii)   After the problems caused by the sudden price rise in the oil sector were successfully tackled, there was a new confidence in developed countries that they could manage their difficult problems in the economic sectors on their own, without the support of developing countries.

(iii) That phase of adjustment brought to them the understanding that there was a need for cooperation among developed countries, whereas cooperation with developing countries was not so necessary. All that was needed was to put the developing countries under constant pressure to keep their markets for exports from developed countries open.

(iv)   The rapid technological development of the developed countries also gave them a renewed confidence that cheap labour of developing countries was not much of a challenge to them, as they shifted from labour-intensive to capital-intensive production of goods and services.

(v) The disintegration of the USSR as a world force also had its important effect in instilling economic, political and security confidence in major developed countries.

(vi) After the initial euphoria of freedom from the colonial regime, most of the developing country governments started feeling the strains of internal problems, and they had to spend much of their time in tackling these problems, leaving very little time for outward attention except to seek support. They could not pose any economic or political challenge to the aspirations of developed countries.

(vii) Over the years, the solidarity of developing countries almost totally disintegrated, and thus there was no threat of any joint challenge from them.

Against this background, the major developed countries have gone on aggressively with their agenda in the economic sectors. There has been stiff opposition from time to time, but at the crucial stage, the points on which major developed countries have common interest are conceded. Of course, the problem still remains in areas where the major developed countries differ.

All this suggests that developing countries have to change their approach and strategy in their interaction with developed countries. Three considerations are important, viz.:

(i) They cannot individually face the developed countries in any serious economic negotiation. Wherever the interests of developed and developing countries coincide, there is no problem, as no resistance or counteraction is needed. The problem arises on issues where the interests differ. And in fact, there are several such important issues.

(ii) They must not expect any special favours from developed countries or any concessions without indicating to them the gains which the developed countries will themselves have in extending the concessions. This could be done either by offering some concessions in the short-term or utilising the existence of the potential of some major long-term benefits.

(iii)   In developed countries, it is the industry and finance, rather than the governments, which are the real operators in the economic sector. Howsoever the governments may be cooperative, there cannot be any useful economic cooperation without the active motivation and support of the firms in industry, services and finance sectors.

There was a time when the governments and the industry in the developed countries were apprehensive about the availability of raw materials from developing countries. Then came a time, when the oil shock faced them with the reality of feeling the brunt of the autonomous policy decisions of developing countries. Now there is no such fear. The developing countries have become somewhat weak and dependent on them in many ways. Raw materials will be available in plenty as the developing countries, having them, need foreign exchange. Oil price rise has been fully taken care of by suitable adjustment which was carried out at great speed and with single-minded determination.

Then the question arises as to what can be the attractive offers from the developing countries' side which could attract the attention of the developed countries. There are two obvious points of attractions, viz., (i) huge consumer base and (ii) vast biodiversity resources.

The growth of demand for industrial goods is bound to slow down in developed countries, because of two reasons: their low economic growth and the low growth of their population. Hence they have to look elsewhere for sustaining their production. The potential in developing countries is enormous. There is a huge population base and existing levels of consumption are low. The levels will rise with economic development, and even a modest rate of rise of demand may result in vast total demand because of the large population base. In fact targeting of this market has already started.

As minerals and agricultural products are losing their importance in developed countries as raw materials, biodiversity resources are coming to the centre stage. The multinationals in developed countries have great need of these resources for their further research, technological development and new production lines.

Developing countries have to realise the importance of these new components of their bargaining strength. These can be utilised by them individually or collectively.

Individual approach is not very potent, particularly in the context of WTO. Combined approach of a large number of countries is effective both as demander and defender. Developing countries have lost their cohesion over the last ten years or so. They have been encouraged systematically to perceive their individual interests as separate from those of others. Whenever there is any sign of cohesion among a few developing countries immediately it is disparagingly described as politicising GATT/WTO.

While making this allegation, it is forgotten that a major effort of politicisation in GATT took place, not by developing countries, but by developed countries, during the UK-Argentina dispute in the Falkland-Malvinas case. At that time, the UK invoked the security provision of Article XXI of GATT 1994, which was quite all right, since the UK was itself a party in the conflict. It was also understandable that other members of the then EEC invoked this provision, since their trade was almost integrated with that of the UK. But almost all developed countries invoked this, though they had hardly any significant economic or security interest in this matter. The invocation was done mainly to demonstrate the political solidarity of the developed countries. It had inspired Argentina at that time to raise the issue in GATT, seeking establishment of criteria for action under this provision.

In fact what is needed is a cohesion of interest of at least some developing countries on a sustained basis, not only on case-by-case basis. It is a big irony that the countries which are individually quite strong have various fora for coordination and they have a good informal mechanism of cooperation even in the WTO, whereas the developing countries which need coordination among themselves have been drifting apart. If all developing countries cannot have full coordination among themselves, at least a large number of them should consider undertaking this exercise on a stable and institutional basis.

The only way for them to be effective in the WTO is to have such coordination. Otherwise, they will be individually pushed around and their interest will be jeopardised. The essential elements of the coordination may be the following:

(i)   intensive consultation and discussions on important issues to evolve common perceptions and, thereby, common demanding and defensive approaches,

(ii)   frequent and periodic exchange of information among them on issues relating to important problems and proposals,

(iii)   regular consultations at Geneva level and at the level of high trade policy officials in the capitals,

(iv)   exchange of studies and reports of non-confidential nature among Geneva delegations and also in capitals,

(v)   wherever interests coincide, effective common approach and strong supportive statements in formal and informal meetings; and wherever interests do not coincide, refraining from open opposition, if such opposition is not absolutely necessary to serve its own interest.

The need of coordination among developing countries is felt more as new proposals for inclusion in WTO negotiations keep pouring in.

Considerable improvement in the WTO system from the point of view of developing countries is possible if some of them, say even ten to fifteen, have full coordination among themselves on a stable basis. Further, if there is political input into this process, economic coordination, particularly in the WTO context, will have a sound foundation.

Summary of Positive Features, Deficiencies and Required Changes

A. ENFORCEMENT OF RIGHTS AND OBLIGATIONS

POSITIVE FEATURES

1. Automatic decision making has been prescribed. Hence there can be no blocking of decisions.

2. Time frame for various stages has been laid down. Hence there will be no undue delay.

3. There is a resulting confidence in the dispute settlement system.

DEFICIENCIES AND IMBALANCES

1. It may take more than two years before a country fully corrects a mistake.

2. In really vital and important cases, the only relief for an affected country may be retaliatory action, which it may not like to take. Hence there may be no real relief.

3. In anti-dumping cases, panels have been given only a limited role, and they are practically ineffective.

4. There is no relief against delays by panels and Appellate Body.

5. The process of dispute settlement is usually very costly for developing countries.

6. The cross-sectoral retaliation is weighted against developing countries.

REQUIRED CHANGES

1.   The time-limit allowed to the panel and Appellate Body should be halved.

2.   The time frame for full compliance with the recommendations should be fixed by the panels.

3.   The erring country should pay compensation to the affected country. The quantum of compensation should be determined by an arbitrator.

4.   If retaliation is to be resorted to against an erring country, particularly if the complaining country is a developing country and the erring country is a developed country, there should be collective retaliation by all Members.

5.   The restrictions on the panels in anti-dumping cases should be removed.

6.   Panel members should be discouraged from undue delay. While choosing a panel member, the past record on adherence to time schedules should be kept in view.

7.   There should be guidance to panels about limiting themselves to the essentials of the case and also about the need for the reports to be brief. Also panels should themselves seek relevant information from various sources, thereby reducing the burden on developing countries in this regard.

8.   There should be a provision for payment of cost by a developed country party to a developing country party, if the complaint or the defence of the latter is found to be correct and if the stand of the former is found to be wrong.

9.   The provision regarding cross-retaliation should be removed.

B. MARKET ACCESS

POSITIVE FEATURES

1.   There has been significant reduction in tariff; and thus market access has improved.

2.   Grey area measures will be eliminated within a time frame; and no grey area measures will be taken in future.

3.   Small suppliers will have a role in negotiations when a country proposes to raise tariffs beyond the bound levels.

DEFICIENCIES AND IMBALANCES

1.   In developed countries, tariffs are still high on products of interest to developing countries.

2.   Tariff escalation still continues in developed countries, with the result that production and export of processed natural products is discouraged.

3.   In the prohibition of grey area measures there is a possible loophole. In the examples of measures, minimum import commitment has been left out.

REQUIRED CHANGES

1.   Tariffs on the products of interest to developing countries should be reduced in the developed countries.

2.   Tariff escalation in developed countries should be reduced and finally eliminated.

3.   Minimum import commitment should be included in the prohibition of grey area measures in future.

4.   There should be positive structural adjustment in developed countries in order to ensure that there are no more pressures in future for introducing grey area measures. Governments of developing countries should work out specific programmes for structural adjustment. The implementation of the programmes should be monitored in the WTO.

C. CONTINGENCY TRADE MEASURES

C1. BALANCE OF PAYMENT MEASURES

DEFICIENCIES AND IMBALANCES

1.　There is a constraint that quantitative restrictions as bop measures can be taken only when it is shown that tariff-type measures are not effective in tackling the bop problem. Thus the discretion of developing countries in the choice of measures has been curtailed.

2.　There is no criterion for the existence of bop problems. In considering whether bop problems exist in a country, the nature of the reserves or that of the inflow of foreign exchange is not taken into account.

3.　There is a provision for public announcement of elimination of bop measures; it does not appear fair. There is no such requirement for grey area measures.

REQUIRED CHANGES

1.　Constraints on the developing countries regarding the choice of measures should be removed. They may take either price-based measures or quantitative restrictions measures as they consider appropriate.

2.　Unstable nature of the reserves or inflow of foreign exchange should not be taken into account in deciding whether the bop problems exist.

3.　If there has not been a public announcement by a country regarding elimination of measures, it should not be insisted upon.

C2. SAFEGUARD MEASURES

POSITIVE FEATURES

1.   The procedure has been well codified, thus subjective actions have been curtailed.

2.   Causal link between the injury and imports has to be demonstrated before taking safeguard action.

3.   Time-limits for continuing the measures and restrictions on repetition of measures have been laid down.

4.   There is a *de minimis* limit for developing countries.

DEFICIENCIES AND IMBALANCES

1.   The provision of quota modulation has risks associated with it. The criteria for departure from the established process of quota allocation have not been laid down. The limits to which departure is allowed have also not been set.

2.   There is no clarity as to how the *de minimis* provision for the developing countries will operate.

3.   The procedure for taking safeguard measures is complex, and there is a risk that developing countries, while taking safeguard measures, may be faulted for not following scrupulously the detailed technical procedure.

REQUIRED CHANGES

1.   Specific criteria should be laid down for adopting quota modulation.

2.   Clear limits should be fixed for departure from the normal quota shares in the process of quota modulation.

3.   There should be effective monitoring of the process of quota modulation to ensure that developing countries are not specifically targeted.

4.   There should be a clarification that the developing countries falling within the *de minimis* limit will not be subject to the raised tariff or quantitative restriction imposed as a safeguard measure.

5.   There should be a decision that procedural deficiencies of developing countries in taking safeguard measures will be ignored if these are merely of technical nature.

D. MEASURES AGAINST UNFAIR TRADE PRACTICES

D1. SUBSIDIES

POSITIVE FEATURES

1.   Procedures for taking countervailing duty action have been made detailed and objective.

2.   The necessity of demonstrating the linkage between the injury and subsidised import will provide protection against frivolous pressures on governments for action against subsidy.

3.   The *de minimis* provision will help developing countries.

DEFICIENCIES AND IMBALANCES

1.   Subsidies prevalent in developed countries have been made non-actionable, whereas those mostly used by developing countries have not got such facility.

2.   The process of initiating action against subsidy as also the defence against anti-subsidy action has become very complex. It can be very costly for developing countries.

3.   Exclusion of countries from Annex VII merely because of a temporary rise in the GNP per capita can be harmful.

4.   Exclusion from special dispensation is automatic if a developing country reaches the level of competitiveness, but there is no automatic inclusion if it again falls below this critical level.

REQUIRED CHANGES

1.   Subsidies on production and export in developing countries necessary for their industrialisation and development should be categorised as non-actionable.

2.   Panels should collect information on their own if these are needed by developing countries in supporting their case in the panel process.

3.   A developing country should be excluded from the Annex VII only when its GNP per capita remains at or above the critical level for two years.

D2. ANTI-DUMPING

POSITIVE FEATURES

1.   Detailed procedures have been laid down, which has improved the objectivity of the process.

2.   The provision of linkage between the injury and dumped imports will discourage undue pressures on governments for anti-dumping action on imports.

DEFICIENCIES AND IMBALANCES

1.   Panels handling disputes relating to anti-dumping have a very limited role, and in this process the dispute settlement mechanism has been made quite ineffective.

2.   The procedure is very much complex. It is very costly for developing countries to collect information from other countries and prepare their cases.

REQUIRED CHANGES

1.   The constraint on the panels should be removed.

2.   Measures to reduce the cost to developing countries as mentioned in the section on subsidies should be adopted here too.

E. AGRICULTURE

POSITIVE FEATURES

1.   A beginning has been made to bring agriculture into the normal disciplines of international trade.

2.   Some major developed countries which were having restrictive regimes of market access and high domestic support will be reducing these measures at least to some extent.

DEFICIENCIES AND IMBALANCES

1.   Those countries which have been keeping high levels of market access constraints, domestic support and export subsidy will be able to continue with a large portion of these practices, whereas those that were not using these measures have been prohibited from having them in future. There is an inherent unfairness in this treatment.

2.   Domestic production will be discouraged and imports will be encouraged, if the domestic production is more costly than imports. This may be dangerous for food items, particularly for developing countries. These countries are often short of foreign exchange and as such their dependence on imported food items will be really dangerous.

3.   Non-commercial farming sector in developing countries, particularly household farming and small-scale farming will suffer greatly. This will have serious consequences for a large section of the rural population in a large number of developing countries.

4.   There are high tariffs in several developed countries as the tariff equivalents of non-tariff measures have been taken to be high. Such high tariffs will result in limited market access opportunities for other countries.

5.   No specific measures have been prescribed to bring relief to the net food importing developing countries, even though their problem has been recognised.

6.   Some studies have shown that several countries have not followed the modalities properly in preparing their schedules.

7.   Some developed countries have mixed the tariff quotas relating to bilateral and plurilateral agreements with those for global allocation and have prescribed country allocations even though some of these should have been open for all countries. This has reduced the market access prospects of other countries.

8.   There is uncertainty about the domestic support, as only overall commitments have been made and product-specific measures will be known only later, perhaps on a year-to-year basis. This puts the outside exporters at a handicap as they are not able to assess the competitiveness of specific domestic products in advance.

9.   In respect of the subsidised food stock of developing countries, the subsidy involved in purchases is to be included in the current AMS. This means, in essence, that there is practically no special dispensation, as developing countries can in any case retain this subsidy by reducing some other subsidy.

10.   In the provision for due restraint, the subsidies prevalent in developing countries usually get less favourable treatment than those in developed countries.

REQUIRED CHANGES

1.   Those countries that have not included in their schedules equivalents of market access restraints, domestic support and export subsidy should not be altogether prohibited from introducing some of these measures in future. They should be allowed to do so up to a certain extent.

2. Developing countries should be allowed measures which will be necessary for them to encourage domestic food production.

3. There should be flexibility regarding the import restraint and domestic subsidy in developing countries to support and protect household farmers and small farmers.

4. There should be ceilings on the peak tariffs in the agriculture sector in developing countries.

5. Modalities for the calculation of commitments should be given some formal recognition. The schedules should be checked up again and corrections should be allowed and, in fact, made necessary.

6. There should be specific enforceable measures for the relief of net food importing countries. Large net food exporting countries should bear the cost.

7. Tariff quotas should be made global, except in exceptional cases where commitments in bilateral and plurilateral agreements have to be respected.

8. Domestic support for specific products should be announced well in advance, for example, for three years at a time.

9. The subsidy provided by developing countries for the purchase for public stocking should be excluded from the calculation of current AMS, as is the case with other permissible domestic support.

10. The discrimination in due restraint between the measures in Article 6 and those in Annex 2 should be removed.

F. TEXTILES

POSITIVE FEATURES

1.   MFA expired on 1 January 1995, and it has been decided to bring textiles fully into the normal disciplines of international trade by the end of 2004.

2.   The transitional safeguard provision is less unfavourable to developing countries compared to the corresponding provision in the MFA.

3.   The role of the TMB has been made strong and more effective than that of the TSB.

DEFICIENCIES AND IMBALANCES

1.   The progressive liberalisation process has been rather retrograde. Major developed countries have been able to fulfil their obligation technically without actually making any real liberalisation. This has been due to the weakness in the Agreement.

2.   The operation of the transitional safeguard has been unsatisfactory. Some major importing countries have been able to invoke this provision with undue severity.

3.   The Agreement contains a strange provision of sectoral balance of rights and obligations. Further, the provision is also weighted against developing countries, since the action for disturbing the balance is lowering of the increase in growth rate of quotas. This punitive provision can only be targeted against the developing countries. There is no corresponding punitive provision in case developed countries are found to disturb the balance.

4.   The end-loading of liberalisation will have serious problems, as the industry in developed countries will be suddenly facing a

major opening of the market. There may therefore be strong pressures on the governments of these countries to continue with restrictions even beyond 2004.

REQUIRED CHANGES

1. In the second stage of liberalisation, the process should advance further than the required level in order to compensate for the absence of actual liberalisation in the first stage.

2. The provision of the Agreement that transitional safeguard should be sparingly used should be properly enforced. The Agreement should provide for some specific ways in which it can be done. One way could be to prescribe compensation for frequent use of transitional safeguard, if the measures turn out to be wrong.

3. The provision of sectoral balance should be removed altogether. In any case the bias against the developing countries should be removed, and thus there should be a balancing provision for punitive action if the balance is disturbed by developed countries.

4. Major developed importing countries should monitor the structural adjustment process in this sector. It should be under the scrutiny of TMB.

G. NON-TRADITIONAL ISSUES

G1. SERVICES

DEFICIENCIES AND IMBALANCES

1.   There is an imbalance between capital and labour in the Agreement.

2.   Provisions for developing countries have not been specifically included in the operative parts of the Agreement.

3.   There is an imbalance in sectors which are identified for priority negotiations.

4.   Sectoral negotiation is quite impractical. Better results can be achieved if negotiations in several sectors are taken up at the same time.

REQUIRED CHANGES

1.   Movement of labour should at least be given the same special consideration as has been given to the movement of capital.

2.   There should be monitoring of the observance of special provisions for developing countries. This can be done primarily in the Committee on Services.

3.   It should be ensured by the Committee on Services that sectors of interest to developing countries are taken up for negotiation on priority basis.

4.   Several sectors should be taken up for simultaneous negotiation.

G2. TRIPS

DEFICIENCIES AND IMBALANCES

1. The objectives of the Agreement on TRIPs have not been incorporated in specific provisions of the Agreement.

2. The Agreement provides for the protection of the rights of the IPR-holders, whereas there is hardly any provision specifically for the rights of the users of IP.

3. The attempt at the harmonisation of minimum level of protection ignores the basic problem that the balance between various interests in the intellectual property in a country depends on the socio-economic background and the development priority of the country.

4. In the field of layout-design of integrated circuits, there is grave risk for consumers. If they happen to buy equipment which contains such a circuit illegally, they have to pay royalty to the IPR-holder.

5. There is a bias in favour of raising the level of protection of intellectual property. It occurs in the provision relating to amendments of WTO Agreements.

REQUIRED CHANGES

1. Specific provisions should be included in the enforceable parts of the Agreement to ensure that the objectives of the Agreement are fully respected.

2. There should be some provisions explicitly in the Agreement to ensure the protection of consumers.

3.   There should be a re-thinking on the process of harmonisation of minimum level of IPR.

4.   If countries utilise the discretion given to them in the Agreement in respect of various features, there should be due restraint in initiating dispute settlement process, even if some countries are dissatisfied with it.

5.   The bias in the process of amendments in favour of raising the level of rights should be removed.